Pedestrian Safety Expert Gets Hit by Bus

Pedestrian Safety Expert Gets Hit by Bus

Another Weird Year of Bizarre News Stories from Around the World

Huw Davies

Cartoons by Knife and Packer

Andrews McMeel Publishing

Kansas City

First published by Ebury Press in Great Britain in 2003.

Pedestrian Safety Expert Gets Hit by Bus copyright © 2005 by Huw Davies. Illustrations © 2005 by Knife and Packer. All rights reserved. Printed in Canada. No part of this book may be used or reproduced in any manner whatsoever without written permission except in the case of reprints in the context of reviews. For information, write Andrews McMeel Publishing, an Andrews McMeel Universal company, 4520 Main Street, Kansas City, Missouri 64111.

www.andrewsmcmeel.com

05 06 07 08 09 TNS 10 9 8 7 6 5 4 3 2 1

ISBN-13: 978-0-7407-5464-7

ISBN-10: 0-7407-5464-5

Library of Congress Control Number: 2005923054

Contents

Introduction

Welcome to another weird year, another catalog of craziness that will allow you the voyeuristic thrill of watching the rest of the world—the mad ones, the ones you have nothing to do with—embarrassing themselves in a variety of ways. You'll laugh, you'll cringe, you'll feel nauseous, you'll roll your eyes to heaven. Above all you'll feel a huge sense of relief that there are plenty of people out there who make a mess of things far worse than you could ever do, even on your worst day.

Now, I've noticed this year that stories in the "Stupid" category have increased slightly over last year. This is completely natural and to be expected. It's a form of social evolution—as technology makes things easier for the majority of people, they simply get stupider. Or rather, denied the stimulus to make use of whatever wits they may have been born with, people are allowed greater scope to express their inherent stupidity.

Yep, being stupid may be inherent—part of a person's genes. This ties in with the statement made by James Watson, one of the two biologists who discovered the structure of DNA. He was recently featured in a documentary about DNA and was of the opinion that stupidity could quite possibly be corrected by gene therapy. "If you are really stupid," he said, "I would call that a disease. . . . I'd like to get rid of that."

I would like you to rally around me in defending your right to read about the brilliance of stupid people. It's your right to know about people testing guns by firing them into a frying pan in front of their face, about an escaped prisoner who changes out of his bright orange prison uniform into something even more noticeable. If stupidity is bred out of humanity, all bank robbers will remember to cut eye holes into their masks so they can see, no one will try to open an aerosol can with something that would light the gases inside, and no one will hijack a vehicle and demand to be taken to where it was already going. Where's the fun in that?

Thankfully, weirdness is not solely a question of human dimwittedness. Animals feature large, and who's going to breed the loopy genes out of them? Then there are the cosmos engineering accidents of all shapes and sizes, many of them weird. And coming back to humans, possibly the only other thing that you guarantee on a mass scale besides rank stupidity is lust. Horniness. Often disguised as love by those too feeble to face the biological truth that raging hormones make for raging weirdness. Men and women attack each other and cut out thousands of paper hearts and sleep in ponds and point shotguns at their private parts, all in the name of love. As they say, love makes the world go weird. And it's all in here and at www.anotherweirdyear.com, where you can read a regular supply of stories and even add your own dippy discoveries. Enjoy.

ANOTHER CRIMINAL YEAR . . .

We begin with a round-up of the strange and surprising crime stories of last year.

A weird paradox. In the tiny state that is home to one of the world's holiest men, crime was discovered to run rife. Vatican City was reported to have crime rates higher than practically any other country in the world, despite being the home of the pope. In fact, the vast number of visitors to Vatican City makes it a pickpocket's paradise, and statistics show that over 87 percent of the population has committed a civil offense, while an astounding 113 percent have committed a penal offense.

USUAL SUSPECTS, SIR

dishonesty and honesty are the best policies

In Equatorial Guinea (that's in West Africa, in case you didn't know) a man broke into his neighbor's house to steal her video and TV. So far, so dishonest. He was mid-theft when the neighbor returned unexpectedly, with a friend, so the man had no choice but to hide. While he was hiding, they started preparing a meal, and he witnessed the "friend" adding poison to the food, whereupon he came out of his hiding place to denounce the friend, who fled. The man's neighbor was so relieved that she gave him the items he had been trying to steal.

Work this one out! Retired British actor Michael Fabian was on trial for harassment and wanted to act as his own lawyer. He contacted an employment agency and got them to send him twelve actors to sit in the gallery. Why? Fabian felt that his defense speech was so theatrical and moving that he could only do it justice in the presence of an attentive audience (even if they were not quite the real thing). However, he skipped town without paying the employment agency, was prosecuted a second time, and got six months in jail.

The audacity! Police in the Brazilian city of São Paulo discovered that there was a fake police station operating in the center of the city a mere three hundred feet from a genuine one. The bogus setup was fully equipped with fake policemen and detectives who charged huge fees for their services. They would have carried on undetected had they not blackmailed two of their "clients"—who immediately went and complained to the real police. A secret investigation was launched and eventually the real police went in and arrested all the fake ones.

Police in Paraguay uncovered a very cunning, if rather disgusting, scam. Thieves were breaking into cemeteries and plundering dead bodies for their teeth. They then sold the choppers to dental laboratories to be made into dentures. A government spokesman called upon the robbers to leave the dead in peace.

A Norwegian, in prison in the town of Stavanger for being a menace to society, was let out briefly, under escort, so he could get married. The wedding went smoothly, and the man was given a few hours with his new bride in a nearby hotel for an early wedding night. Not only did he consummate his wedding, but he took his new wife with him as he sneaked out of the hotel and held up a local shop, before being caught again. Not bad for a day in the life of a prisoner: release, wedding, consummation, armed robbery, arrest, and back inside.

The best ideas are often the most obvious. After that it's all a matter of the quality of execution, which was where Swede Mikael Persson let himself down. The stroke of genius was to steal coins out of parking meters in the city of Gothenburg with a vacuum cleaner. The mistake was doing it in broad daylight. The sight of a man holding a vacuum cleaner to a parking meter did not go unnoticed, and the police

like father, like sin ODD

A jury in Pennsylvania gave the verdict that Landon D. May, twenty, was to receive the death penalty for two murders he committed in 2001. He ended up on death row, where he was reunited with his father, Freeman May, who was there following his own conviction for murder shortly after the birth of his son. Landon broke into the house of a school principal and his wife, together with the couple's adopted son, and stabbed, shot, and strangled the couple. His father, Freeman, had stabbed a twenty-two-year-old woman to death in the early '80s, but he wasn't caught and convicted until the body was found and identified much later.

were on to him in a flash. Persson had just cleaned up at one meter and was weighed down with $300 worth of coins when he was stopped and carted off.

HATE CRIME

A man in Los Angeles got the shock of his life when he received a taped-up parcel containing a deadly snake that could have killed him. Joseff Calhoun opened the box that arrived by post to discover a two-foot-long black-necked spitting cobra. This cobra, which not only has a lethal bite but can also spit venom up to a distance of nine feet, was clearly no Valentine's Day gift. Calhoun shut the box before the cobra could wriggle out, and police were brought in to attempt to trace the sender. The cobra was taken to the Los Angeles Zoo and Calhoun said he had no idea why anyone would want to send him a deadly cobra, although he had received a "vague threatening letter" a few months earlier.

Possibly the most pathetic crime that came to our attention over the last year was this one. A Russian man—a grown-up, apparently—in the town of Ulyanovsk made a hoax bomb call. His target was a public spa, the day was a women-only day, and his tragic motivation was that when the police went to evacuate the building he would see lots of naked women running out onto the street. As if. Yes, the women were evacuated and, no, they didn't all run out naked. Surprise, surprise, they all put on clothes. Our very mature criminal, meanwhile, faced a little spell in prison for his efforts.

And the most pathetic near-crime was this one, courtesy of the Choking Man. The Choking Man, who at the time of writing had not been tracked down, is a short, fat—actually very fat—balding man with a moustache; not the most attractive man in the world. His scam has been to pretend to be choking in the vicinity of attractive women in Punta Gorda in the hope that they will minister to him. Thrashing his arms around, coughing and spluttering, Choking Man just has to be rescued. And when a pretty woman "saves his life," well, he's grateful, isn't he, and smothers her with kisses and big hugs. There's no actual crime involved, although one woman went to hospital with an anxiety attack after being "thanked" by him. Another woman who "rescued" him used the Heimlich maneuver, holding him by the waist from behind (he must have *loved* that!), positive that he was choking to death on the apple he had been eating. Finally, when one of the rescues was reported in the local paper as a genuine life-saving attempt, several women recognized Choking Man's description and phoned in to tell their own stories. Suddenly it all became clear.

worst choice of getaway driver

When police in Chile foiled a robbery, they discovered that the driver of the getaway car wasn't really qualified for his job, in that he had no arms and no legs. His knees were tied to the steering wheel, and he worked the pedals using sticks that had been attached to his neck and elbows. Apparently he had learned to drive using a Formula One simulator.

One of the silliest crimes involving threats and ransom demands was this: Gary Lee McMurray, thirty, of Tennessee, phoned Debra Letourneau while she was visiting someone and told her that he was in possession of her upper plate of false teeth and that if she didn't pay a ransom, he would step on them. McMurray was arrested for grand larceny. The amount of the ransom he demanded was not disclosed.

SNOW CONES

An ice-cream man in the Chilean city of Valparaiso was caught selling some of the "special stuff." The thirty-five-year-old had been mixing cocaine paste into chocolate ice cream and was selling the naughty cones alongside other flavors, with a guarantee that they would "get you high." Unfortunately for him, an off-duty policeman, quite unsuspecting, bought one of his "specials," then sent a few plain-clothes colleagues to get just a little more proof before making an arrest.

MURDER MOST WEIRD

A German actor had a fight with his tax consultant and ended up killing him. Nothing *too* unusual in that, but it was the method of murder that fascinated us. When the argument—in which fifty-five-year-old obese Günther Kaufmann (weighing 270 pounds) attempted to blackmail his consultant—reached fever pitch, Kaufmann crushed Hartmut Hagen underneath him and suffocated him, for which he received a fifteen-year prison sentence. A bit like going to Fat Camp, really, only for longer.

EATEN UP BY CRIME

Prepare yourself for what is possibly one of the most gruesome crime stories of the year—or ever, come to think of it. A forty-one-year-old German confessed to the murder of a man who answered his advertisement on the Internet in which he asked to meet a man who would be willing to be killed and eaten. The man, living near Kassel, reportedly video-taped the encounter with his willing victim. Police searching the murderer's house found several tapes recording his actions, as well as a freezer containing remnants of the victim. The act of "sex cannibalism" began, by mutual consent, with the victim having his penis cut off and then cooked so that both men could taste it before the act of killing took place. The organ was reportedly flambéed, then tasted, found to be lacking a little something, then fried to improve its flavor. Then the older man made a series of deep cuts in his companion's neck to kill him, and, with the videocam still rolling, chopped his corpse up into pieces, which he froze and later ate.

The world of rap is populated by some strange people, yet none stranger than Antron Singleton, also known as "Big Lurch." The Texan rap artist, who has performed with stars such as Mystikal, was discovered wandering the streets of Los Angeles naked and covered in blood. Not his own blood, as it turned out, but that of a woman he had murdered. When the woman's body was found, her chest had been torn open and it looked as though her lungs had been chewed; tests on Singleton found flesh in his stomach that was not his own. The rapper was charged with murder.

More gruesome stuff for the ghoulish amongst you: Joey Cala, a Texan, beat to death his seventy-nine-year-old mother, then cut her open and ate part of her heart. According to Cala's sister, Joey wanted their mother's money. However, this did not seem to be his motive, since there was nothing to suggest that she had much money at all. Furthermore, when he was discovered by a police officer standing over the freshly killed body of his mother, covered in blood and with part of "an organ" in his mouth, he accused the officer of having interrupted his satanic ritual sacrifice.

taken for a sucker

A Thai man waiting at a bus stop in the town of Nakorn Ratchasima was approached by two attractive women who asked him if he wanted to go back to their room for a bit of fun. Needing no further bidding, he soon found himself being treated to a close-up view of the women's breasts as they took off their tops and urged him to suck their nipples. Since the women had coated their nipples with a sleeping drug, that was the last thing he remembered before passing out. He woke up later, alone and robbed of all his cash, his jewelry and his mobile phone. He did have a smile on his face, though!

SEXY

Finding herself in financial difficulties, the owner of a tea shop in the Chinese city of Haidian hit upon a cunning idea to boost business. She placed an ad in the local paper saying that she was seeking a lover. She then arranged to meet the respondents in—yes, her own tea shop. With the lust-crazed suitors guaranteed to pay for her in the hope of something more, she would order the most expensive items on her menu, then make an excuse to leave early. As is so often the case, she pushed it a little too far and got caught: One prospective lover cheekily asked for a discount off his bill, and she had her kitchen staff beat him up.

CAR-BASED CRIME

An Italian man, forty-year-old Andrea Cabiale, was arrested for fraud and harassment after it was found that he had purposely caused at least five hundred car crashes in his home city of Turin. The harassment? Cabiale's trick was to disable his car's brake lights, then stop suddenly in front of a woman driver he had previously targeted so that she would crash into the back of his car. He would then suggest an informal settlement, take the woman's telephone number, and proceed to harass her over the phone. The unemployed Cabiale managed to make enough money from the trick to buy property in the ultra-chic French town of Cannes.

A police unit in the Welsh town of Llanelli took on the name "The Frying Squad" when they operated "Stop, Sniff, and Search" checks on hundreds of drivers in the town. A widely adopted practice of buying cooking oil, adding a dash of methanol, and using it in place of fuel for diesel cars was saving drivers hundreds of pounds in fuel costs—the only catch being that it was illegal. The local Asda supermarket was selling so much cooking oil that it was forced to introduce rationing as owners of diesel cars bulk-bought, fueling their cars for around 60¢ per litre (as opposed to the forecourt price of diesel at $1.40). And as one driver who had been caught admitted, his car ran as sweetly on the cooking oil mix as it ever did on diesel. The fatal drawback was that the fuel gave off a very distinctive smell, so undercover police officers could hang around the town center, sniff the fumes of passing cars, and then stop the driver. A quick dip into the fuel tank would reveal the crime of using illegal, untaxed fuel, and in the case of the driver above, all his savings went to a thousand-dollar fine and three-hundred-dollar costs for having his vehicle impounded. So don't try this at home, diesel-owning readers.

Dutch police near Arnhem pulled over the driver of a car reported as stolen and arrested him. It turned out he was on his way to court to answer

Car-based crime with a difference! Ray Wilson planned his great crime in his local library. Having read up on how to drive a forklift truck, he then hot-wired a $50,000 Caterpillar forklift in his home town of York and tried to drive it to his mother's house in Liverpool. There followed a bizarre car chase at speeds of up to 25 mph as Wilson succeeded in keeping his police pursuers at bay for an hour, even lifting their "stinger" road traps out of the way with the forks, as well as driving on the wrong side of the road, knocking cars out of the way, and terrorizing pedestrians. Eventually he collided with a police van on the busy A64 road to Leeds, still a long way from his mother's house, and was arrested.

charges of stealing cars—and since he didn't actually possess a car, he simply stole another. "I don't have a car myself, I just steal and sell them," he told them, quite reasonably.

Another story about a miserable young man stealing an unfeasibly large vehicle to go and see his mother. A Russian soldier stole an army truck and broke out of his base at Vatutinki, one hundred twenty miles south of Moscow, by crashing through

ODD

Police officers arrived at the scene of a road accident in Belarus where a car had just been wrecked, according to the two men who called them out. Now, these two men were lying: The car was old, and they wanted to collect the insurance for it, so they had smashed it up and towed it out to the spot where they claimed it had been involved in a crash. It all would have gone according to plan if the two men hadn't looked so . . . well, unconcerned about such a nasty accident. The police officers smelled a rat and looked under the hood. No engine. The cunning plan was not so cunning after all, and the two men were taken away by those clever policemen.

the gates because he was missing his mother. His fatal error was to drive into Moscow "to see the capital" on his way home. He got embroiled in a high-speed chase that lasted an hour, ending with his arrest.

A South African motorist with no driver's license took a slightly skewed view of the rights of married couples by telling police who stopped him that everything was in order because he had a right to use his wife's driver's license. And he was so convinced that he was in the right that he produced his marriage certificate there and then. The motorist received a hundred-dollar fine for driving without a license and his wife was fined for allowing an unlicensed person to drive her car.

DIVINE RETRIBUTION

When God calls upon animals to do police work.

Two men robbed the Rhino and Lion Reserve in Krugersdorp, west of the South African city of Johannesburg, holding up the cash desk at the entry kiosk and then running off with the cash in opposite directions to confuse pursuers. One man climbed into a waiting car and was whisked away, while the other acrobatically scaled a high fence and dropped to the other side—straight into the tiger section of the reserve. The tigers fell upon the robber, swatting him around and playing with him as cats do, and he died of a broken neck and fractured skull. The tigers had to be sedated before the body could be removed.

Oswaldo Martinez, accused of murdering judge Harmodio Mariscal while attempting a robbery in Panama City, fled to the neighboring country of Costa Rica but was captured and jailed. Undaunted, he broke out of jail and tried to get home to Panama. He fought his way through dense jungle to the banks of the River Terraba so that all he had to do was cross the river to be home and dry, so to speak. But fate intervened in the form of a crocodile. As Martinez was swimming the river he was eaten alive.

STUPID CRIMES

Criminal geniuses these people are not. Nor are they masterminds who can dream up the perfect crime and execute it, cleanly, clinically, and coolly. No, these guys execute their crimes stupidly, stupidly, and stupidly.

When you're under age and desperately need an ID to get into a bar, what do you do? Some Australian schoolboys from Toowoomba in Queensland knew the score: They used school equipment and a computer to produce forged driver's licenses, which Queensland's licensing minister, Merri Rose, later pronounced as "high-quality fakes." The fatal flaw? The moronic mistake? The boys were wearing their school uniforms in the photos, which gave the game away to bouncers at the bar they were trying to get into. The forgeries were confiscated and the police notified.

Now, where do we start? Edward Blaine, sixty-one, qualifies for the stupid criminal section first of all because he's already served a twenty-year stretch for bank robbery. So what was he caught doing? Robbing a bank, that's what. But it gets worse (or stupider). Blaine robbed a bank in Virginia and was escaping with the booty—$100 notes were falling out of his pockets as he ran, which didn't help things. He arrived at his getaway car and realized he'd locked the keys inside it. He grabbed a log to smash the window but then threw it away in anger. The log hit a passing truck, and the enraged driver, Emmett Lowe, grabbed his gun and chased Blaine. There was a struggle, and Blaine tried to shoot at Lowe but hit himself in the leg; seconds later Lowe fired, hitting Blaine in the same leg.

Pride comes before a fall. Arrogance and stupidity come before an arrest. John Thomas Boston, thirty-nine, had been on the run from police in Louisville, Kentucky, since 1994. He had succeeded in getting to the Canadian border, and to rub the police's noses in it, he mailed them a letter telling them that they would never catch him. This year he was arrested in Dallas and charged with three rapes from 1994, since he had left plenty of DNA on the envelope when he licked it.

Edward Green, twenty-four, arrived **DAFT** at the sheriff's station in LaPorte, Indiana, to bail out a friend and ended up being arrested himself. He was told to take a seat for a moment, and promptly fell asleep. (Note: It's just possible that there may have been alcohol involved at some earlier stage.) After a while, a deputy went to wake him and his eye was caught by a strange sight. Green's mouth was hanging open as he snored, and several small plastic bags were visible inside, which were later found to contain cocaine.

A little bit of forward planning always helps, but then that requires a little bit of intelligence, something that was clearly not part of Masood Dawali's criminal character. The twenty-five-year-old burst into a bank in Giessen, Germany, pulling a mask over his face as he did so. He then stumbled around the bank, crashing into customers and walls as he fumbled his way to the counter: He hadn't cut eye holes in his mask! In order to demand the money, therefore, he had to pull off his mask and look straight into the security camera, so that he was fairly easy to catch once he'd fled. He didn't get any money, by the way. They told him that the safe couldn't be opened, and anyway, they weren't really very scared by his plastic knife and toy pistol.

Hijackers traditionally want to go to Cuba; well, the weather's nicer there, isn't it? But a hijacker in London used a very cunning ruse to get to his destination. The man, in his fifties, jumped onto a double-decker bus, produced a gun, and ordered the driver to take him to Bromley (an area of London). The driver pointed out, perfectly reasonably, that the bus was going to Bromley anyway. The hijacker held his gun to the driver's head and told the driver to drive on and not stop at any lights or junctions until he got to the Bromley police station. On arrival, armed police boarded the bus and arrested him.

Shoplifting in supermarkets is pretty risky, what with all those security staff and closed-circuit cameras. So drawing attention to yourself after you've carried out your theft is a bit stupid, yet this is exactly what a twenty-five-year-old Italian man did in the town of Saronno. He swiped a frozen chicken drumstick and hid it in the front of his under-pants while he waited in line. Slowly but surely the agonizing cold got to his tender parts and he was observed by the cashier to hop around while touching the front of his trousers. She called security and he gave himself up, probably with some sense of relief.

Drive-by shootings are a fact of life in Los Angeles. Occasionally, though, the gang members get it horribly, stupidly wrong. A twenty-two-year-old man driving the car involved in a drive-by attack was killed when his passenger shot at his intended victim out of the driver's window. The bullet never reached its target because it hit the driver first.

Okay, so you're aware that prisoners have to wear uniforms that make them easy to spot if they should ever get on the wrong side of the fence. At the prison in Waco, Texas, for example, inmates wear bright orange jumpsuits. They don't look cool, but you know exactly who they are. One such orange-clad fool, Timothy Baker, escaped while serving a sentence for aggravated robbery. He holed up in nearby Baylor University, where he raided a building to find some less noticeable clothes. Only trouble was, the building happened to be the Fine Arts Center, and Baker went straight for the costume wardrobe. Casting off his conspicuous jumpsuit, he put on a nineteenth-century bright green wool costume with rubber galoshes. According to the local sheriff, who had him back inside before you could say "inconspicuous," he looked just like a leprechaun, and stood out by a mile.

 Insurance fraud drives our premiums up, so it's good to see that one potential fraudster didn't let intelligence stand in the way of being found out on the spot. A Dutch woman went to the police station to report that her skis and a very expensive pair of ski trousers had been stolen while she was on holiday in Austria. As she described the trousers it became apparent to the police officer that they were the ones she was wearing—she had forgotten to take them off. She later confessed to attempted fraud.

YUCKY CRIMES

Some criminals have no sense of delicacy or decency. A man who carjacked a Honda Civic outside a large shopping mall in the Canadian city of Edmonton left behind something that no one was keen to pick up and return to him—his colostomy bag. The man, waving a knife, had tussled with security guards at the Bay Mall before jumping into the Honda. In the struggle his shirt was torn loose, and so was the colostomy bag beneath it. The man drove off, evading capture, and despite a massive search, remained out of the police's clutches. If they needed DNA, though, they had a bag full of it.

One victim of unhygienic practices among the criminal classes was Falkirk police station in Scotland. It became infested with fleas that arrived with a prisoner. Several officers and support staff in the control room were bitten but bravely soldiered on, protecting the people of Falkirk from crime (but not from fleas). Pest-control experts were brought in, and a police spokesman went on record as fearlessly saying that despite the infestation the station was operating normally.

Yucky crimes or cunning liars? Decide for yourselves: Two men in the Belgian city of Antwerp were in court on accusations of drug dealing because they had bought bulk supplies of boric acid. The prosecution's case was that boric acid is added to cocaine before the drug is sold on the streets, and the huge quantity of boric acid bought by the two men was evidence that it was going to be used in drug dealing. The two men, however, both Moroccans, told the judge that their wives had sent them to the chemist to buy the stuff because their feet stank so badly that they were unable to stand it, and that boric acid was the foot-odor remover of choice in the Moroccan community. After listening to both sides, the judge believed the stinky feet story and the men were acquitted.

SEXY

GENEROUS CRIMES

Last year we had criminals who broke into houses and left things there. This year?

Jacqueline Boanson of Cheltenham has her debit card stolen. Boo-hoo. Next, $600 mysteriously appears in her account. Hurray. Andrew Cameron had stolen Ms. Boanson's debit card and used it to put two $100 bets on the horses with bookmakers Ladbrokes. He backed winners—hurray—and Ladbrokes paid the winnings directly into Ms. Boanson's account. Boo-hoo (for Mr. Cameron).

In Tacoma, a woman was about to be raped and began to pray out loud. Her attacker stopped and asked her if she was a Christian, to which she said yes. He then apologized, pulled up his trousers, and went away.

AN ASSORTMENT OF UNUSUAL CRIMES
Self-punishing crime

Remorse can be a powerful emotion, and, as this story shows, it can drive people to weird extremes. A thirty-six-year-old Romanian man, who had committed the very slightly wicked crime of stealing some wood from a forest, was so overcome by guilt and remorse that he tied himself to a cross, sewed his lips together, and put a barbed-wire crown on his head. Then, clad only in his underpants, he dragged himself across the village to the police station to turn himself in. He was eventually fined $40 for public order offenses while the wood theft was under investigation. So not a lot of forgiveness there, then.

Cheeky crime

It was worth a try. . . . Wesley Fitzpatrick, of Kansas, applied to a Kansas City judge for a temporary restraining order against a woman he said was stalking him. Fitzpatrick said she made him "scared, depressed, and in fear for my freedom." The judge granted the order, but when Fitzpatrick appeared in person to make the order permanent, it turned out that his stalker was in fact his parole officer! Close, but no cigar. Fitzpatrick was immediately arrested for not having met her as he was supposed to.

Community of crimes

In a recent census, every single resident of the Bangladeshi village of Jahanpur listed their occupation as "thief" (and they weren't joking). As a result, politicians demanded that they all be evicted, so police had to cordon off the whole village.

Starving crime

A Japanese man's attempted bank robbery collapsed in failure—because he collapsed from hunger. Yukiharu Akamine, thirty-nine, walked into a branch of the Tokyo Unity Bank in Itabashi-ku and stuck a kitchen knife into the counter. That was about as far as he got, as he then collapsed. He had been living on water for a month, having lost all he had through gambling. After he was arrested, police provided him with a square meal and apparently he cheered up immensely.

Crime inspired by standard cartoon practice

Wile E. Coyote—or maybe Daffy Duck—may well have taught Jimmy Tran a thing or two. Tran, of Plainville, Connecticut, sawed through the ceiling of his own apartment and the floor of the apartment above his, where a woman lived, and tried to steal her handbag by reaching through the hole he had made. Unfortunately for Tran, the woman was at home, and his pathetic and visually highly amusing attempt was swiftly foiled.

STUPID COPS

Gross stupidity is not just the province of criminals. . . .

At 1:30 A.M. a policeman interrupted a group of men removing furniture from a warehouse in Middlesbrough, UK. Neighbors who had spotted the men opening a steel roller door and backing a four-ton truck into the warehouse called the police. When the officer arrived, the men told him that they had a set of keys and were just moving the furniture. Satisfied that this was the truth, the whole truth, and nothing but the truth, our genial bobby told them to keep the noise down and drove off. The thieves got away with $50,000 worth of goods.

I hope that I'll still be exercising when I'm in my nineties, but clearly I'll have to be on the lookout for stupid policemen, especially if I move to Norway. Ninety-four-year-old Sigrid Krohn de Lange was stopped by police in the Norwegian town of Bergen while she was out jogging. The reason? They were convinced that she had escaped from a nursing home and couldn't believe that she was just . . . exercising. Sigrid had a heck of a job persuading the ageist officers that it was part of her regular exercise routine, and was even forced to give them her address so that a police officer could check that she really lived there. They eventually let her carry on with her run.

An Austrian police officer started the night shift at his police station in the town of Leibnitz drunk, so drunk that he decided that what he really wanted was peace and quiet, and none of those annoying emergency phone calls asking for help. So he slashed the telephone cables and switched off the radio set, leaving the station uncontactable. He was charged with criminal damage, suspended from duty, and fined $2,000.

Abusing their power? Policemen? Never! Well, hardly ever . . . Patrick Shields, a police officer in Pensacola, Florida, came across a courting couple in their car one evening. He threatened them with arrest for indecent behavior but told them he would overlook it if they were to do a quick set of exercises. He made them both do jumping jacks, barechested. Fine for the boy, but more than a little humiliating for the girl, especially as he was shining his torch on her as she bounced up and down. After they complained Shields resigned, having twice refused to take a lie-detector test.

Oversensitive cops

A Canadian man was arrested in Vancouver for carrying and not eating an iced bun. Police became convinced that he was going to throw it at Prime Minister Jean Chrétien during a walk-through in the city, based on a rumor that someone in the crowd was intending to "pie" him. William Christiansen, who was carrying the bun, was asked by a policewoman what he was going to do with it, to which he replied that he was going to eat it. When the policewoman asked him to eat it then and there, Christiansen declined—he didn't want to eat it with her watching him. And that was enough for Constable Danielle Efford, who arrested him on the spot. At the same time, another man suffered the indignity of having his car towed away on the grounds that the trunk may have been full of cakes. Cameron Ward was told that he matched the description of a suspected pie-thrower. He said: "I was never charged, never processed, and I was held in an awful, awful place for hours. It's outrageous. I can assure you I have not visited a bakery within the last forty-eight hours."

GIVING THEM MORE THAN THEY BARGAINED FOR
Cool as f**k

We are in awe of the cool presence of mind of a man attacked by would-be car thieves at a filling station in Indianapolis. The two robbers accosted him as he was filling up his car, but he simply pointed the gas hose at them, drenching them in gas and sending them sprinting in terror for safety.

You can just imagine the expression on the face of carjacker Tyrone Jermain Hogan, twenty, of Los Angeles, when he held up a nice big van that he liked the look of only to find that inside the van was the martial arts team from a university in Florida. Hogan didn't stand a chance and was swiftly pinned to the ground while the police were called.

PRISON BREAKOUTS

Those Basques are very cunning. A member of the separatist group ETA was spirited out of one of France's toughest (supposedly) jails by his brother, who did nothing more than switch places with him during a visit. Ismael Berasategui Escudero had been linked to a massive weapons haul found in southwest France earlier in the year and had been arrested after being caught in possession of a loaded gun. His brother came to visit, they switched places, and Escudero walked free, while his brother, who bears no more than a family resemblance, went inside, waited a few days, and then revealed his identity to embarrassed

Vietnamese fish sauce? Ever tried it? It's fermented, so it's more than a bit whiffy and strong—the sort of stuff you'd think could probably eat through metal. Which is just what some of the inmates at the An Binh Centre in Vietnam's capital Ho Chi Minh City thought. Twenty-six men, heroin addicts in enforced treatment, used the fish sauce to rust the bars, then used guitar strings to cut through them. They had heard that their treatment program (jail sentence) was to be extended, so they wanted out, and their cunning use of a very smelly condiment brought them success. **UNUSUAL** officials. He was placed in custody, but the damage had been done and his brother was well away.

Now we're not saying that some prison guards are easily distracted from their task, but there was a bit of a mess at Kotido prison in northern Uganda when thirty-one inmates were at work in the prison garden, watched over by five guards. You'd think this would be a fairly healthy guard-to-prisoner ratio, but when a rabbit appeared from under a bush and hopped off with the guards in pursuit, the prisoners ran off, too, unsurprisingly.

Clearly, Ugandan prisons aren't the toughest in the world. Fifteen inmates escaped from the Kigo prison, near the capital, Kampala, by using urine to weaken the prison walls. Over a period of time, they peed with great accuracy on a single spot on the wall, then used spoons and metal bars to dig through the wall while the guards were asleep.

You go to jail, you escape, and years later you find yourself in the same jail. One thing you wouldn't expect, though, would be to escape through exactly the same hole you got out of eleven years earlier. But that's exactly what happened to David Ivy, who got out through a hole in the fence at the Shelby County jail in Tennessee, which had not been repaired since he'd used it in 1991.

PRISON LIFE

Prison life isn't supposed to be pleasant, but sometimes prisoners protest against certain conditions that they find too difficult to bear. In Kazakhstan, forty-three inmates of the Aktubinsk penal colony were fed up with having to attend compulsory lectures on socio-legal matters and wanted more freedom to move around the colony. Their bizarre protest was to simultaneously attempt ritual disembowelment on themselves using shoe horns. No one actually spilled their guts, and we don't know if their pleas were listened to.

Robert Paul Rice, serving a sentence in Utah state prison, filed a lawsuit demanding that the prison accommodate him as a vampire by providing special vampire meals and conjugal visits that would allow him to partake in the "vampiric sacrament"—by which he meant drinking blood. Unfortunately for Mr. Rice, an appeals court turned him down, and a prison spokesman went on record to say that no one gets conjugal visits in Utah, blood-drinking or otherwise.

Inside, prisoners have a code of conduct, but those heartless, thoughtless criminals on the outside don't adhere to it. So it must have been tough for the inmates of Spring Hill prison in Buckinghamshire when thieves broke in and went on a stealing spree. They stole cash from inmates' lockers, mobile phones, and $1,000 from a safe—money earmarked for discharge grants for released prisoners.

THE LAW

A decision that Bill Clinton would surely heartily approve of: At an annual judicial conference, Taiwanese judges voted 49–11 that oral sex, without intercourse, should not be legal grounds for adultery.

Leon Humphreys, of Bury St. Edmunds, attempted to invoke an ancient right to "trial by combat" rather than pay a $50 fine. Mr. Humphreys, sixty, had failed to notify the Driver and Vehicle Licensing Agency (DVLA) that his motorcycle was off the road, and so was fined. He refused to pay, instead offering to take on a clerk from the Swansea-based agency with Samurai swords, Gurkha knives, or heavy hammers. Magistrates sitting at Bury St. Edmunds court rejected Mr. Humphreys's request to do battle with the DVLA's champion in a fight to the death and fined him a further $400 with $200 costs.

Mothers-in-law: can't live with them, can't use them as grounds for divorce. Well, now you can, according to an appeals court ruling in Italy. A woman from Vasto, in southern Italy, was granted a divorce after years of excessive interference in her married life by the mother of her husband. He was, according to the woman, his mother's slave, doing everything she told him to, while the mother criticized everything about her daughter-in-law: her diet, her makeup, even the way she was bringing up the couple's daughter. After the ruling the woman was awarded custody of the daughter, while the husband went home to live with mama and save up for his alimony payments.

THE PETTY ARM OF THE LAW

Dogs—they bark, pant, chase sticks, come in various shapes and sizes, all instantly recognizable. Guinea pigs—don't bark, don't pant, don't look anything like dogs. It's fairly clear-cut, isn't it? However, the wardens of the Carl-von-Weinberg Park in Frankfurt weren't going to let a trifling detail like correctly identifying an animal stand in the way of some really top-class pettiness. They fined a man the equivalent of $450 for letting a guinea pig run free in their park. The fifty-seven-year-old man, who was looking after the pet for his daughter, was in breach of a law that bans dogs without leads, and although he took the trouble to point out the difference between a dog and a guinea pig, the wardens paid no attention. And to cap it all, the poor guinea pig also received a life ban from the park.

In the UK, the law says that drivers are supposed to try to avoid hitting dogs, but not cats. And rabbits don't even come into it. In Romania, on the other hand, police actually fined a motorist for running over a rabbit. Nicolae Balaita was fined $20 (sounds fairly light, but it was the equivalent of a week's wages) after he hit and killed the rabbit near the town of Adjud. Mr. Balaita said: "I hit the rabbit because there was no way for me to avoid it." His car's bumper was damaged by the impact, so he went to a police station to report the incident. When the animal-loving officer saw the rabbit's blood on the car, he became angry and handed out a fine. The police stood by their decision, saying Mr. Balaita had clearly been speeding.

Bus stops at bus stop, passengers get off, others get on, bus drives away. A straightforward scenario that takes place possibly millions of times a day the world over. It's one of those things that no one really pays any attention to. No one, that is, except for an over-zealous traffic warden in Manchester. Taking the idea that a bus stop was a restricted parking area and running with it a little too far, he wrote a $75 parking ticket on a number 77 bus that pulled in to set down and pick up passengers, who looked on in disbelief as the warden told the bus driver that no one was allowed to park there, not even buses. Manchester City Council later apologized and canceled the ticket.

It was a major operation: Police staked out the scene of a terrible crime in a bid to catch the yogurt-pot dumper of Donauwörth in Germany. Street cleaners had complained to the police that someone had been dropping a banana yogurt pot and a spoon on the grass median every day, week after week, month after month, and year after year. So the police lay in wait for the repeat offender and the waiting game paid off. The police operation netted the super-criminal, a fifty-five-year-old truck driver, who was fined $500 by the city and ordered in the future to put his yogurt pot in the bin . . . and the little piece of aluminum foil from his sandwiches that he used to cram into the bottom of the yogurt pot to weigh it down, the better to throw it from his window out onto the grass.

WHAT NOT TO WEAR— IN A COURT OF LAW

Two assistant district attorneys at a hearing in a murder case in Louisiana, where the death penalty is operative, turned up to court wearing ties decorated with a hangman's noose and the Grim Reaper. Donnie Rowan and Cameron Mary were rebuked for their "joke" and told not to do it again.

LAWSUITS

Shifting the blame, making a fast buck, complaining, and whining—are these the only uses for a court of law? The US carpet adhesive company Para-Chem puts a very clear warning on its product that reads: "Do not use indoors because of flammability." Not a lot to misunderstand there, is there? The idea is not to use this adhesive indoors. And that would be understood by professional carpet-fitters, too, assuming they could read. Well, we're not saying the law is an ass, but the Para-Chem company was ordered by a jury in Akron, Ohio, to pay a massive $8 million to two professional installers who were badly burned in an explosion when they—you can probably guess the rest—used the adhesive indoors. One juror said he and his colleagues felt the warning did not go far enough in convincing the installers not to use the product indoors.

Last year twenty-one Brazilian magicians successfully sued the country's largest TV network for loss of income after a series of programs that revealed the secrets behind magic tricks. Exposed to the public were such standards as pulling a rabbit out of a hat and sawing a woman in half, and the court agreed that interest in magic shows had diminished as a result of the series. TV Globo was ordered by the court to reimburse the magicians, some of whom claimed to have lost up to 70 percent of their income thanks to the series. Presumably it was easier for the magicians to sue than to learn a few new tricks.

In the city of New York a thirty-eight-year-old woman decided to end it all by lying down on the track in front of a subway train. As sometimes happens, she wasn't killed, but was badly maimed. Who should get the blame for her injuries? Why, who else but the train driver, of course. It apparently didn't matter in the least that the driver had slowed the train to 15 mph after hearing a report that there was someone on the track, in order to avoid a death; the jury found that the train was still going too fast, and awarded the woman over $14 million. The judge later reduced this amount to just under $10 million on the grounds that the injuries were "30 percent her fault."

Jacqueline Morrison, a train driver for the Scottish firm of ScotRail, filed a lawsuit against her employer for around $30,000 following her life-threatening injury—a bruised fingernail—sustained while adjusting her seat in the cab. Now you may think that's an outrageous sum of money to claim, but to be fair, the fingernail did eventually drop off.

There's win-lose, and there's lose-win: An Australian was in a fight at school, threw the first punches, but lost the fight when he got knocked out. Seven years on, however, he won big time when he was awarded about $700,000 from a lawsuit in which he claimed that life had been physically and financially tough for him ever since.

It's a well-known phenomenon, isn't it? You get slapped with a raw steak and wallop! You stop fancying your partner. No? You don't identify with that? Well, that's what Tim and Donna Vogle claimed happened to them in a restaurant in St. Joseph, Missouri, after Donna complained that her steak was overdone. The restaurateur apparently came out and slapped Mrs. Vogle in the head, and in the subsequent lawsuit the couple asserted that their sex life had been diminished by 75 percent. **QUIRKY**

It's amazing how much value some people place on their love life. In the case of June Bond, thirty-four, of Ventura County, California, that value was $300,000. Her husband, while on a work program for violating his probation (probably in order to be closer to his loving wife), stamped down a palm frond into a rubbish bin and it snapped back, severing his ear. Naturally this caused a drop-off in matrimonial affection that was worth, according to the suit filed against Ventura County, $300,000. Maybe because her nibbling his ear had become just too painful.

Optimism must positively ooze from Josephine Bailey of West Virginia. She filed a wrongful-death lawsuit against the owner of Rick's Pub in the town of  Hurricane, and against a trucking company, for the death of her twenty-two-year-old son. He had been in Rick's, drinking all night. He had then left, staggered across the street, and collapsed under a large truck standing with its engine idling. The truck driver pulled away soon afterward, having no idea that a man was lying beneath his vehicle, and Ms. Bailey's son was killed. She sued on the basis that her son would never do such a stupid thing, so it must have been someone else's fault (but don't blame the parents).

With many of these stories it's all too tempting to begin with "Only in America . . . ," but this one really fits the bill. Randy Burcheon, of Belton, Texas, is suing himself for $250,000; except he's not quite suing himself, he's suing Larry, who's ruining his life. Confused? So are Randy and Larry! Mr. Burcheon, a tax accountant, suffers from a multiple personality disorder, and five of his six personalities are decent, normal people. But the sixth, Larry, is an alcoholic bully who causes trouble and ruins everything good in Mr. Burcheon's life. It's been going on for ten years, and Mr. Burcheon wants an end to it. He claims that Larry sexually harasses his girlfriend, shouts out obscenities during important meetings, uses his credit card to buy thousands of dollars' worth of booze and to fund visits to strip clubs, and subscribes to German porn magazines. Larry even wrote a string of threatening letters to the president, prompting an angry visit from the Secret Service. Now, as you might expect, Larry, drunken rascal that he appears to be, is not taking this lying down. He vigorously denies the allegations against him and has hired his own lawyer to defend him in court. It's going to be tough, though, since all five of Mr. Burcheon's good personalities have agreed to testify against Larry, and if he loses, the money will have to come from his insurance policy.

We can only wonder at the type of people who were on jury duty for this lawsuit in Ohio. Maggie Smith and her two adult children won $1.2 million in a wrongful death suit against their doctor, Franklin Price, concerning the death of Mrs. Smith's husband, Lawrence, from a heart attack at the age of fifty-four. Mr. Smith, a lifetime smoker who was obese, ate a poor diet, did little exercise, and had diabetes and high cholesterol levels, was also stressed at work. Mrs. Smith's suit claimed that Dr. Price did not do enough to help Mr. Smith avoid his fatal heart attack, despite the fact that he warned him constantly about the dangers of his lifestyle. And somehow the jury— possibly consisting of overweight diabetics in stressful jobs—concurred.

Cherise Mosley, nineteen, filed a lawsuit against a family planning clinic in Houston for the abortion it performed on her two years earlier when she was a minor. In order to get the abortion without her parents finding out, Mosley had used a forged ID card to show she was over eighteen. Two years down the line, she started to regret the abortion, and whose fault was it? Well, not hers, you can be sure. Mosley decided it was all the fault of the clinic, who should have spotted that fake ID, told her parents, and persuaded them to talk her out of it.

This story could just as easily fit into the "Parents" section as here. Anita Durrett stole a cartload of groceries from an Albertson's store in Woodinville, Washington, and sped off in her car, her nine-year-old daughter in the passenger seat. The groceries were worth $266 and an employee from the store promptly gave chase. Durrett lost control of her car at 90 mph, and her daughter was killed. Durrett was convicted of vehicular manslaughter, unsurprisingly—but she herself filed a lawsuit against Albertson's for wrongful death on the grounds that they shouldn't have been chasing her in the first place.

Just like Jack of beanstalk fame, a Russian man got more than he bargained for when he planted some seeds. Nikolay Salakhov, from Pavlov-Posad, near Moscow, sued a seed firm after he was knocked unconscious by a giant pumpkin. The instructions on the packet said he would get something the size of a pear, but the plants that grew from the seeds produced massive pumpkins weighing 40 pounds, one of which broke off and fell on his head as he lazed on his balcony.

THE LAW'S AN (ANIMAL-LOVING) ASS

If you run a business in Boulder, Colorado, you really have to walk the politically correct talk. The Whole Foods Market company was boycotted by animal rights groups when a dead mouse was found in its warehouse, suggesting that this unspeakably cruel and callous company may not have been using rodent-friendly catch-and-release traps.

An animal rights group tried to persuade a town in New York State to change its name from Hamburg to Veggieburg. The People for the Ethical Treatment  of Animals (PETA) offered to supply local schools with $20,000 worth of non-meat burgers in return for the name change, but officials in the town didn't take up the offer. This was apparently not PETA's first attempt to find animal suffering in an innocent place-name: In 1996, the group proposed that the town of Fishkill change its centuries-old name to Fishsave, since they believed the name carried violent images of dead fish.

The same name-obsessed group also approached three Scottish villages, all called Ham. The councils were each offered $10,000 to change their names to Veggie.

Back once again in the city of Boulder, if you live in a certain mobile home park, the end of summer can be pretty crappy. This is the time when thousands and thousands of starlings arrive, festooning the mobile homes with gallons and gallons of their droppings. But residents are obliged to put

up with it all because caring city regulations forbid even shooing the birds away.

Animal rights activists were right behind a decision made by Judge Frederick Weisberg in Washington, DC, when sentencing forty-nine-year-old John Hardy; women's rights activists would have been less enamored of the decision, however. Hardy was involved in a "domestic," getting into a disgraceful scuffle with his wife when their pitbull terrier decided that he wanted a piece of the action and joined in the fight, whereupon Hardy stabbed him fatally. Judge Weisberg gave Hardy three months in jail for assaulting his wife and twenty-four months for the attack on the dog.

ANIMALS FALLING FOUL OF THE LAW . . .

In India, Anurag Rastogi, a magistrate of the Gurgaon district, near New Delhi, issued an order forbidding the assembly of four or more pigs.

This story is not a load of bullsh*t: Prosecutors in Bulgaria really did put a bull on trial in court for murder. The case took place in Kardzhali, near Sofia, after the body of a farmer, Dimitar Chonov, was found trampled to death in the bull's stall.

Apparently it was a way of ruling out any other suspects in the death, and a spokesman for the defense said that there were extenuating circumstances, as the bull had just been given a vaccine that had made it very angry. There was no word as to what the sentence would be if the bull was found guilty.

It was reported that two guard dogs at a prison in Serbia fell foul of their bosses by not barking while five inmates were escaping. The prison officials were chillingly brutal in their punishment of the non-barking guard dogs: They carried out an execution with guns.

How these animals are supposed to find out about these laws, we don't know, but in Montana, officials in Fremont County passed a resolution that forbade the presence of grizzly bears within the county boundaries.

. . . AND THE LAW FALLING FOUL OF ANIMALS

Transport police officers in Vitebsk, Belarus, had to lock themselves in their patrol car when a huge bear ambled out of the forest as they stood on the road near their small police station. While the policemen took cover, the bear first sat on the car roof for about an hour, then went into the police station and ate the officers' lunch and dinner. It then wandered back into the woods, leaving the cops safe but very hungry.

Sheep attacks pig

New Zealand has a sheep population so huge that there are three for every human—of course, the good-looking ones go first. Jokes like that (yes, that was a joke) are commonplace in New Zealand, so when reports were heard of a police officer handcuffing a sheep, it could have been for all the wrong reasons. Fortunately, this is not a sordid story at all; police were called in to deal with a loose sheep at a farm in Dunedin. When they arrived, the sheep, a ewe, panicked and ran into a garage (perhaps she'd heard all the jokes). An officer followed her in and she attacked him, ripping his trousers and leaving him limping. His colleague then wrestled the sheep to the ground and handcuffed the ewe's legs together. To add to all this, it then turned out that they had forgotten the handcuff keys, so they had to call out another policeman to release the sheep.

Animals

CREATURE CRAZINESS

Coinciding with the opening of one of the world's most prestigious dog shows, the Westminster Kennel Club Dog Show in New York City, the United Arab Emirates put on an animal show in Abu Dhabi— a beauty contest for camels. The total prize money was over $30,000.

A zebra foal stumbled into a doctor's front door in Nelspruit, South Africa. The two-month-old foal was blind, hence the stumbling, but the amazing coincidence was that the doctor happened to be an eye specialist. Dr. Danie Louw diagnosed cataracts and immediately arranged for the zebra to be operated on at the local hospital. Shortly after the operation the little zebra was seen back out there with its mom. Aw.

In these days of extra awareness of the plights of endangered species, trying to help animals in difficulty seems the natural thing to do. So when six manatees beached themselves in Palm Beach,

Florida, well-meaning rescuers immediately started pushing them back into the sea. Big mistake! The manatees were females who were in season and had stranded themselves on purpose. The poor females were exhausted from the amorous attentions of a "mating herd" of male manatees and needed a little time out. The last thing they wanted was to be pushed back beneath the waves to be jumped on by the nearest randy male manatee. Fortunately, local wildlife agents were able to step in and stop the do-gooders from condemning the females to more manatee mating.

Next time you tuck into some octopus, spare a thought for the creature—it was probably far cleverer than you thought. Proof? Look no further than Frida, an octopus at the Hellabrunn Zoo in Germany, who has learned to open jars of shrimps by watching her attendants. She presses her body onto the lid and then twists herself to remove it. Aquarium boss Frank Mueller taught Frida the trick so she could do it at feeding time when people were watching, but patience may be required, because if the lid is a little tight, it can take Frida up to an hour to unscrew it.

An unlikely rescue was carried out when a seal was spotted saving the life of a drowning dog in the town of Middlesbrough. An injured German

 Bears killed three motorists in Russia and injured dozens of others on the road between the cities of Adler and Krasnaya Polyana. This wasn't some safari park scenario where idiotic visitors climb out of their cars to get better photos and get mauled to death. The motorists were victims of rock slides caused by bears rolling rocks down the mountainside. The local bears had somehow discovered that they could kill cattle this way, and simply moved on to humans. According to a local hunter, the bears did it for fun.

shepherd had panicked and leapt into the River Tees, where it was swept away on the outgoing tide, yelping in anguish. The noble seal popped up and swam around the dog, sizing up the situation, then pushed it through the water toward some mudflats before modestly swimming away.

SQUIRRELS

It looks as though the world's squirrels were unhappy with the amount of coverage they got in last year's edition of *Another Weird Year*. So they have sprung out of the trees and into action to make up for it. . . .

A squirrel in Germany terrorized a ten-year-old girl and even succeeded in shepherding her up a tree. Lisa Fremmel, of Krumbach, had climbed onto a low branch of a pine tree when a furious squirrel appeared and tried to bite her foot. Afraid of the noisy, aggressive creature, Lisa tried to escape it by climbing farther up the tree, but the implacable beast of doom followed her higher and higher. When poor Lisa was thirty feet up the tree and unable to climb any more, she burst into tears (always a useful tactic) and the squirrel leapt away to another tree, leaving Lisa stuck, unable to climb down by herself. Her tears and cries attracted a passerby, who called emergency services, and the fire department promptly came to her rescue.

fbi squirrel

UNUSUAL

Police in Bath arrested a man on suspicion of burglary when they were called out to a garage where he had been spotted, clearly up to no good. They took him away and returned to the garage to see if they could find concrete evidence of his crime. A gray squirrel sitting in front of the garage ran off a short distance, then looked back to check that the officers were following. They did follow, and the squirrel led them to a tree, around the base of which the booty had been stashed. The squirrel was rewarded with a handful of nuts.

Misguided squirrel

The kindly actions of a tree trimmer in the German city of Hamburg saved the life of a squirrel that had gotten things badly wrong when it came to storing nuts. Toward the end of winter, the man noticed the squirrel in its nest, dangerously thin and surrounded by metal nuts and bolts it had been taking from a nearby construction site. He took the creature to a vet, who saved its life with intravenous fluids and a bowl of fruit.

Flesh-crazed squirrel

Residents of the Cheshire, UK, town of Knutsford lived, for a while, in fear of a gray squirrel of unheard-of savagery. The far-from-cute critter drew blood from six people in a week, biting a woman on the ankle, leaping onto the head of a little girl and biting her eyebrow—her mother had to hold her down and pull the squirrel off—and even chasing one woman around her garden. Although the RSPCA was called in to deal with the violent and voracious rodent, the grand-father of the little girl took the law into his own hands. Armed with an air rifle he stalked the fearsome beast back to its lair in a copse and shot it dead.

Squirrel suicide saboteur

A squirrel with a grudge did tens of thousands of dollars' worth of damage to a high school in Hopkinton, Massachusetts. During the school holidays it chewed through a wire in a transformer, shorting out power to the school and electrocuting itself in the process. After the power cut, the school's sewer pumps failed and water backed up in the system and overflowed onto the wooden floor of the gymnasium, totally ruining it. David Phelan, in charge of buildings and grounds, found the squirrel with its fur sticking up on end and its paws crossed on its chest, having passed on to the next world with the satisfaction of a sabotage job well done.

Water-skiing squirrel

Lou Ann Best has a squirrel named Twiggy who caused a stir at a boat show in Virginia. Lou Ann trained Twiggy to water-ski, following in the footsteps of her late husband, Chuck, who had successfully taught ponies, poodles, an armadillo, and a toad to water-ski. At the boat show, Twiggy rode a specially made set of skis around the twenty-four-foot, six-inch-deep pool, and even wore a life-jacket.

hippos

Farmers in an Ethiopian village were suffering the loss of cattle at the rate of one cow a week. The poor beasts were being devoured—but not by any of the typical predators of the region. The bloodthirsty culprits were the local herd of hippos, who had apparently developed a taste for beef. Normally herbivorous, these hippos baffled wildlife experts, who referred to the cow-eating as a "bizarre phenomenon."

Speedy hamster

Day-trippers on the seafront at Cleveleys, near Blackpool, UK, were astonished to see a hamster in a drag-racing car. He was handed in to the local police, who passed him on to the RSPCA, who promptly confiscated his car. The car is a kind of mobile exercise wheel, and it was assumed that a young hamster-owner had been playing with Speedy, as he was christened, on the seafront and then forgot him, leaving him driving busily up and down. Speedy found a new home when his story made the local papers and a sympathetic hamster-lover offered to take him in.

DEALING WITH DRINKING

A study on the Caribbean island of St. Kitts in which alcohol was given to monkeys revealed startling similarities between the ways in which humans and small primates react to alcohol. The study, involving one thousand green vervet monkeys, showed that the vast majority drank moderately, choosing to have their alcohol diluted with fruit juice and drinking only in the company of other drinkers (and never before lunch). Around 15 percent drank heavily and frequently, preferring their booze as strong as possible, while roughly the same percentage either abstained or hardly drank at all. And about 5 percent turned out to be binge drinkers, knocking it back as fast as possible, getting into fights, and then passing out.

During a heat wave in China, the bears at a Shanghai zoo became addicted to Coca-Cola. Not only did they prefer the great taste of Coke, but they started rejecting plain water. The bears stood on their hind legs and begged Coke from tourists—but bottles of mineral water were angrily flung away after they tasted it.

QUIRKY WEIRD Unusual BIZARRE Strange odd

FISH

New to the US is a fish that seems to have come off a Hollywood B-movie set rather than from its native Thailand. It's called the northern snakehead fish, and a couple were released into a pond in Maryland. Since then this scary fish has multiplied at an alarming rate. It has the head of a snake and the body of a fish, and can breathe air, spending up to three days on land moving about in search of food. The fact that its flesh is very tasty—it is regarded as a delicacy in Thailand—means that at least it'll be worth hunting down if you see one. Just don't let it get its fangs into you. . . .

Sturgeons. Crazy name, crazy fish. Well, the name isn't really that crazy. And usually sturgeons are a very calm, reasonable sort of fish, mainly because they have no natural predators. Last summer in Florida, though, on several occasions, sturgeons of around five feet in length jumped out of rivers and wrought havoc on the poor anglers who got in their way. Injuries sustained by the fishermen included a cracked sternum, broken ribs, collapsed lungs, broken teeth, and lacerations. Why did the sturgeons do it? In an incisive analysis of sturgeon psychology, a local wildlife expert said it was, "Because they can."

A heartwarming piece of fishy news leaked out this year when a report came through of a German angler who has shared his bathtub with a giant eel for thirty-three years. Paul Richter caught the eel in a canal in 1969 and brought it home in a bucket for dinner. But his children refused to let him cook it, so the softhearted Mr. Richter put the eel in the bath for safekeeping, where it has remained ever since. The eel was named Aalfred ("Aal" is German for "eel"), and when his owners want to use the bath they put a bucket into the water and Aalfred swims right into it. The children left home a long time ago, but Paul and his wife, Hannelore, regard Aalfred as one of the family. And since eels have been known to live into their eighties, he may be around for some time yet.

URBAN FARMING

"Indoor pets" are fairly common these days, that is pets that live in blocks of apartments and rarely or never go out. But indoor livestock? In the Turkish city of Trabzon, a woman had been causing something of a nuisance to her neighbors for several years. Fatma Kocaman kept cows in her apartment block. According to reports she had "a large number" of cows in apartments on the first and third floors of the block, and Trabzon's Health and Safety officials had to step in to point out that keeping cattle in an apartment block wasn't something they'd be prepared to accept. Fatma finally gave in to demands and started selling off her housebound herd.

ANIMAL MYSTERIES

Shortly after the deer-hunting season began in the state of New York, a hunter made a perplexing discovery: a deer lodged at least twelve feet up a tree. Later examinations revealed that the deer had been killed by an arrow—the death would have been almost instantaneous—and then put in the tree. But when state conservation officers tried to remove the deer from the tree, they discovered that the fork of the tree in which it was resting was very narrow, making it clear that whoever had put the animal there had in fact lifted it much higher in order to push it downward and wedge it into the fork. The creature was so firmly lodged that officers had to cut down the tree, then pull the deer five feet along the trunk until the fork was wide enough to allow the carcass to be removed. Lifting a deer twelve or maybe seventeen feet off the ground and wedging it perfectly in the fork of a tree is almost certainly beyond the capabilities of the average human, however, especially a lone hunter. So who (or what) on earth could have done it? A hoax is thought to be unlikely—out in the mountainous wilderness of upstate New York it could go completely undetected. Other cases of animal carcasses discovered at a similar height in trees have been reported on many occasions in the US, usually in association with Bigfoot sightings. . . .

Another unusually elevated deer story, this time from Canada, and this time not up a tree. Just outside the city of Winnipeg, a deer was spotted at the top of a telephone pole next to a set of train tracks. Bizarrely, the animal's hind legs were both severed. The best theory—or at least one that does not include aliens playing tricks or Bigfoot tidying up carcasses where no one will trip over them—is that the deer was hit by a train, hence the severed legs, and at the same time catapulted high up into the air, landing by chance exactly on top of the pole. Either way, it's a bit spooky.

When Allan Galliford noticed a little tuft of hair in the middle of the head of one his new calves on his farm in Onoway, Alberta, Canada, he thought nothing of it. One month later, he noticed it was growing into a horn, a third horn, in the middle of her forehead. He decided not to dehorn her as he would normally have done, and when she was a year old this incredibly unusual horn was longer than her other two. No one locally has ever seen a cow with an extra horn, and there is speculation that it could

Could a horse be ridden so hard that it sweated blood? Last year horse experts and specialists from all over China convened in the northwestern town of Urumqi to debate the mysterious "blood-sweating" thoroughbred horse. Scholars argued whether this fabulous horse, famed for its peculiar blood-colored sweat, was in fact a particular breed or whether the mysterious blood-sweating was due to a rare disease caused by parasites that could attack any horse. No final verdict was reached, not surprisingly, although it was acknowledged that the horse did fit the general description of a very ancient and hardy breed, of which three thousand are said still to survive in central Asia.

grow to gigantic proportions, possibly enabling Mr. Galliford to lop off the two normal horns and show the cow as a unicorn. Or maybe a unicow.

Tales of a mysterious turtle in a lake in Vietnam's capital, Hanoi, were long thought to be just that—tales of a mythical creature. The stories date back about a thousand years, but now it seems that they were true all along. Hoan Kiem Lake is home to the world's largest and rarest freshwater turtle, a magnificent giant measuring nearly seven feet from nose to tail. Seen only once or twice a month, the turtle can stay underwater for days at a time. According to Professor Ha Dinh Duc, who has spent a decade studying one of nature's most elusive creatures, it may be a unique species and there may be just this one left, so it could be on the verge of extinction.

FIGHTING BACK

Learn from these tales of courage: Just because you are being attacked by a vicious beast whose only desire is to rip you to shreds and then eat you, there's no need to meekly give in.

David Parker was walking along a remote road in the north of Vancouver Island, Canada, when he was attacked from behind by a cougar. The sixty-two-year-old managed to reach into his pocket, despite being mauled around the head, and grab his small folding pocketknife. Showing amazing tenacity, Parker first killed the big cat and then walked, badly injured and bleeding profusely, over half a mile to a logging area, where workers got him to a hospital.

A pleasant, cooling dip after a hard, hot day's work turned into a horror scene for Mac Bosco Chawinga, forty-three. Mr. Chawinga was swimming in Lake Malawi in the northern district of Nkhata Bay to cool off when he was attacked by a crocodile. The crocodile clamped its jaws firmly around Mr. Chawinga's arms, completely engulfing them in its mouth. With his arms immobilized and his legs flailing helplessly in the water, Mr. Chawinga used the only weapon left—his teeth. He bit down on the crocodile's nose, one of the few soft parts of a crocodile, with such force that the huge reptile immediately released him, and he was able to reach the safety of the shore, where he lay in a pool of his own blood before fishermen found him and took him to a hospital. Adrenalin fuels some pretty astonishing human feats, but even so that must have been one hell of a bite.

SNAKES . . .
. . . can eat dogs . . .

A woman called the police upon discovering a huge snake under the basement steps of her home in Ohio. When the massive python, measuring ten feet, came out, it had a rather large bulge in its middle, a sure sign that it had been feasting recently. One X-ray later a dog that had been reported missing by a nearby resident was found—inside the python.

. . . but they can't eat deer . . .

Not all pythons get it right, however, and sometimes they bite off more than they can chew. A fourteen-foot python died in northern India after swallowing an eighty-eight-pound cheetal deer. Hundreds of people gathered to watch the hugely bloated snake, which was unable to sleep for five days and barely able to move. The overstuffed reptile eventually died, and doctors at Rishikesh's government veterinary hospital, who performed a postmortem examination, said it was because "it had eaten something beyond its digesting capabilities."

. . . and they aren't allowed to eat puppies . . .

Matthew Patton, a biology teacher at Bluestem High School in Kansas, keeps two boa constrictors in his classroom. Sometimes he feeds them during class so that students can see how they eat and digest their food. Usually they get rats and mice. However, a member of the school board who runs an animal shelter donated three unwanted puppies that would otherwise have been put to sleep, and Patton planned to feed them to his boas. Unfortunately for the poor snakes, there were sufficient complaints from parents about the live puppy-eating display that it had to be canceled. The puppies met their end in the shelter, and the snakes missed out on a big treat.

. . . but they can cause a lot of trouble . . .

In Iran, a snake was caught by an eagle. We don't know which of the sixty species of snake native to Iran it was; it may have been the saw-scaled viper, the Mediterranean cat snake, or perhaps even the horned desert viper. Whatever it was, it was one hell of a fighter—first it broke free from the eagle's talons as the bird soared above a road in the province of Khorassan, and then it dropped into a car. It went on to bite four passengers: Two died there and then; two others made it to the local hospital, where they were treated for their wounds.

. . . and they need care, too

A Californian king snake was rushed to the vet in Lydney, Gloucestershire, after it got into difficulties while giving birth. One of the eggs it was laying got stuck—don't laugh, it wasn't funny for the snake—and the vet's nurse had to take a deep breath and pluck up her courage before administering the kiss of life to the dying reptile. The snake, named Nipper, was non-poisonous, but had bitten its owner on more than one occasion, so for nurse Claire Farina to put her mouth upon the snake's required dedication indeed. Luckily for Nipper its breathing restarted, and luckily for Claire she didn't experience its fangs being sunk into her lips.

ZOOS

Animals are supposed to be safe in zoos. Isn't that the whole point?

Zoos often have petting sections for the kids where rare breeds of domestic animals are kept. In the German town of Recklingshausen some of the animals in the pet zoo went missing and the finger of suspicion eventually pointed at two zookeepers. Unable to resist the temptation of having such a rich source of food so close, the dastardly keepers had slaughtered and barbecued five Tibetan mountain chickens and two Cameroonian sheep. Their actions may have left a bitter taste in their mouths, as they were sacked.

Intruders broke into the Krefeld Zoo in Germany and liberated a leopard from her cage. Whether it was for a joke or a misguided attempt at giving the leopard a better quality of life, we do not know. Either way, the leopard, named Katrin, went straight to the kangaroo enclosure and had a feast. An expert said afterward that the kangaroos' hopping would have set off Katrin's hunting instincts. No, really? She managed to kill ten 'roos before she lost interest, and was found the next day lying queasily among the corpses, probably promising herself she'd go on a diet.

WILD BOARS

A wild boar on a rampage in western Germany rammed the front door of a house belonging to an elderly couple with such force that it flew open. The boar charged into the house and upstairs into the couple's bedroom and leapt into bed with them. He bit the man and then left as quickly as he had arrived, leaving the couple very shocked but with no serious injuries.

Undoubtedly realizing what his fate was to be, a 240-pound boar escaped from an abattoir in Dunblane, Scotland, and holed up in the hills. "Big Black," a French boar, struggled with the slaughterer and proved the stronger before clambering over a five-foot wall and crossing a river to reach some woodlands. The Central Scotland police were called

out to help but were unable to bring the boar back to face the meaty music. As news of "Scotland's Most Wanted Pig" began to spread, vegetarian TV stars Martin Shaw and Jenny Seagrove offered $800 for the poor porker, double the market value, to save him from the sausage scenario. Eventually a deal was made to take the boar to an animal sanctuary, so Big Black's efforts to make a break were well rewarded.

A heartwarming boar story from the heart of rural France: A ten-month-old boar turned up one day at the farm of André Vieillard in the Normandy village of Fleury-la-Foet. Its mother had, it was assumed, been killed by hunters, and the youngster had been trotting around searching for her. He was adopted by Monsieur Vieillard's herd of cows and was being fed by them—the cows had to lie down to enable the boar-calf to suckle. And as far as the farmer was concerned, the baby boar was welcome to stay until he was old enough to strike out on his own again.

Some boorish behavior from a couple of Romanian boars, who caused havoc in two seaside resorts on the Black Sea. One, in the resort of Mamaia, broke windows and ran through the foyer at a hotel, terrorizing guests. The second struck fear into the hearts of holidaymakers on the beach at Constantia, emerging from the sea and causing the lifeguard to shinny up a tree to save himself.

WEIRD SURROGATES

In the state of Maryland, a twenty-two-day-old piglet found an unusual surrogate mother when he snuggled up to a terrier who had never even had puppies. Amazingly, when Dallas, the potbellied piglet, started suckling, Dusty, the terrier, started producing milk! The two animals took such a shine to each other that they played together all day long, Dallas firmly convinced that Dusty was his mom.

A little village in eastern India was the scene of a phenomenon that astounded all the locals. A thirteen-month-old boy was refusing his mother's milk and crawling instead to the house of a neighbor to suckle from the udder of a cow. Hundreds of people flocked to the village to see this for themselves, lining up to worship both the child, named Rahul, and the cow, who fed the little boy despite the fact that her own calf was not getting enough milk.

Muemue, a fallow deer fawn, was born in a game park in Hungary and was attacked by the other animals in his enclosure. One of the keepers took pity on the poor deer and took him home, where a mother greyhound also took pity on him, feeding him and nursing him along with her own puppies. It wasn't long before the keeper was treated to the awesome sight of the speedy fawn leading the pack of young greyhounds in warp-speed gallops around the garden.

FLYING COWS

In the last book we had two flying cow stories. And cows were still taking to the air this year. . . .

When Norwegian Olof Kalstad called police to say that he had narrowly escaped being crushed to death in his car by a cow, they hurried to the scene in order to secure this obvious lunatic and get him to a hospital. They were more than a little surprised then to see the bovine corpse only inches in front of Olof's car. He had been driving along a mountain road when he saw a large shadow ahead of him, and very quickly realized that something massive was falling from the sky. Olof braked sharply, just in time to see a cow plummet from the mountainside onto the road. Police later said that if the cow had landed on the car the impact would probably have killed Olof. And no one ever worked out quite how the cow got airborne—perhaps it was a bovine suicide.

In the Austrian countryside near Salzburg a woman was hospitalized after an errant cow strayed onto the road using the route drivers are least likely to expect—the arial route. The thirty-six-year-old woman, with her husband in the passenger seat, suffered chest and foot injuries when a cow that had wandered to the top of a tunnel entrance fell off it just as the woman's car emerged beneath. The cow was killed; the woman's husband was unharmed.

Back to Norway, where flying bovines seem to be nearly as common as sparrows. Not a cow this time, but an elk. Cars often hit elk in Scandinavia, but elk hitting cars doesn't happen quite so often. Leo and Else Henriksen were driving along in southern Norway, admiring the view, when a 770-pound elk landed on the windshield of their little Mazda 232. Leo was a bit peeved to see his windshield wrecked and, worse, as the elk then slid backward along the roof of the car, his ski box was swept away by the huge beast's body. Leo and Else were fine, suffering only a few cuts and bruises; the elk was struck by another car as it lay in the road and was killed.

WHEN ANIMALS ATTACK
It's a jungle out there. . . .

Surprise!

In China, alcoholic drinks containing preserved snakes are extremely popular. But no, that's not the weird news story—there's more. A man named Li uncorked a bottle of booze in which a snake had been pickled for a year and lifted it to his mouth. However, the snake, which had somehow survived its year-long immersion, slithered out of the bottle and promptly bit Li in the neck, proving that alcohol makes you violent. Li was taken to the hospital but was not hurt.

In Australia there is a modest, unassuming brown snake called, with typical Aussie simplicity, the brown snake. It is, however, deadly poisonous, and has amazing powers, too, if this story is anything to go by. When Queenslander Dennis Carr found a brown snake in his garden, he sliced its head off with a spade. When he went to dispose of the apparently lifeless severed head, it bit him on the finger. Seconds later he collapsed; his wife immediately called for medical help and his life thankfully was saved.

"If I die, you die," was the philosophy of a pig on a farm in Minnesota. The final act of the pig, clinging to the last thread of life, was to see off one of its slaughterers. Two men were getting ready to butcher the hog. One of the men shot it with his .22 rifle, whereupon the dying beast lurched into him, pushing his hand onto the trigger and causing him to shoot and kill his colleague.

Bats. They're bats. And they live in bat caves. So after you've read this story you'll know to avoid a certain cave complex in Anyuan county in the eastern Chinese province of Jiang-xi. Liu Ding-yuan had been close to the mouth of these caves, talking on his mobile phone, for about fifteen minutes when he noticed a black cloud in the distance, approaching rapidly. The cloud was actually over one hundred bats, attracted by the ultrasonic signals from his phone, and they dive-bombed Liu, leaving him with face and head injuries.

BIZARRE

Cockfighting is no longer a favorite blood sport in the UK, but it is hugely popular in the Philippines, where vast sums of money are bet on fights, as roosters equipped with steel spikes slice each other to pieces. In the town of Zamboanga, though, things went more than slightly awry as a rooster picked on the wrong adversary. Just as his handler was about to release the bird into the fighting arena, it turned and flailed its razor-sharp steel spikes at him, catching him in the thigh and groin and slitting him open. Bleeding profusely as a massive crowd of stunned sports fans looked on, the man was dead before he even reached a hospital. There must be a moral to that story.

Poetic justice? Raymond Poore, Jr., of Winchester, Virginia, called his wife at work to say he was going to beat their dog to death because it had bitten him. When she got home she found him suffering from a gunshot wound to the stomach as well as covered with dog bites. Poore had been beating their shar-pei with his own shotgun, holding the barrel and using the butt as a club. The gun was loaded, though, and the impact of the blows eventually caused it to go off. He died later in hospital, while the dog survived.

A weird tragedy occurred in Phoenix, Arizona, when a babysitter put her charge, a three-month-old baby girl, down for her afternoon nap in a crib. Half an hour passed, and the babysitter went in to check on the infant, to find her completely covered with black ants and having great difficulty breathing. By the time emergency services arrived she was dead, probably because of the huge number of bites she had received.

MAN'S BEST FRIEND . . .

What about this for doggedness? A young black Labrador dog-paddled for ten miles through the waters of the Solent between the Isle of Wight and the mainland, dodging ferries, oil tankers, and yachts, to reach land after falling overboard from his master's boat.

Two-year-old Todd's six-hour ordeal ended when he swam up the River Beaulieu in Hampshire and made dry land. Police identified him when they scanned the microchip in his ear.

How Dosha, a dog in Clearlake, California, survived one fateful day is beyond us—but she did. First she was hit by a car. When a police officer came to the incident, he decided to put the dog out of her misery and shot her in the head. As far as he was concerned, she was dead, and her "corpse" was taken to an animal control center and dumped in a freezer. A few hours later one of the center's officials went to the freezer to dispose of the body and noticed that she was still alive. Very cold, but alive.

They say animals are creatures of habit, but Yvonne Stubbs's Jack Russell had a habit that was far from normal. Patch was taken in by Yvonne and her eighteen-year-old daughter—both smokers—and from day one at their home in Middlesbrough he started raiding their ashtrays for cigarette butts and chewing them up. Then he started begging for cigarettes whenever one of them sat down for a smoke, preferring to chew up the tobacco and spit the filter out. Yvonne's next move, she said, would be nicotine patches—for the dog, that is, not her.

. . . and worst enemy **MAD**

If your car is your best friend, then these dogs are your worst enemy. A frenzied pack of large "boxer-like" dogs attacked six parked cars in the German city of Munich at about 4:30 one morning in a kind of canine dawn raid. As well as damaging the cars, they instilled panic in those residents who were woken up by the disturbance. Bumpers, mudflaps, and license plates were ripped off, and afterward the cars were covered in teeth marks, saliva, and blood from the dogs' mouths. One witness, gazing out anxiously from behind his curtains, saw a dog launch itself repeatedly against the side of a car, while another resident found that the mad pack had ripped the bumper off his wife's VW bus, causing over $1,000 in damage. Experts could give no reason for the dogs' bizarre behavior.

A dog's best friend . . .

Jim and Susan Jovanovic were celebrating their seventh wedding anniversary at a riverside restaurant when suddenly Jim leapt up from his seat, charged through the emergency exit, and, still dressed in his smart anniversary celebration suit, dived into the river. Jim had been watching the river (after seven years of marriage maybe there was a lull in conversation) and saw a dog floundering in the river, clearly in distress. Going under twice with the disoriented and rather heavy dog, Jim eventually managed to haul it to safety, to the huge relief of its owner, who bought the couple a bottle of wine in the restaurant. With Jim drenched to the skin, though, they had to put their celebration dinner in a doggie bag and take it home.

. . . and worst enemy

You'd have to be really drunk not to be scared of a big police German shepherd that's being set on you. And even more drunk to bite it in the throat. That's what happened in the town of Syracuse in New York, where Paul Russell, Jr., was thrown out of a bar by bouncers. As police arrived with the scary dog in tow, Russell was lying on the pavement where he had landed, presumably feeling bitter and unloved. As the dog came up to him, he grabbed it by the throat and bit it, and a police officer had to use force to haul him off the dog. Asked later about this classic "man-bites-dog" scenario, Russell replied that he had been far too drunk to remember anything. So that's how drunk you have to be. . . .

Who's a clever dog, then?

Gordon Husband always throws sticks for his collie, Shadow, to fetch when they are out for walks. Occasionally, though, Shadow brings back something other than the stick. Like when Husband threw a stick onto the bank of the River Wye in Hampton Bishop, Hereford, and Shadow returned with a live grenade in her mouth. Husband carefully eased it from her mouth and carried it home, then called army bomb disposal experts, who blew up the grenade. He had mistakenly assumed it was a dummy training grenade, so he was more than a little surprised by the huge bang, and extremely thankful he hadn't carried on playing "fetch" with it.

IT'S A DOG'S LIFE

This enterprising German artist must have read last year's *Another Weird Year* (he claims this idea is the first of its kind, but a close reading of *AWY* shows that a Brazilian pet shop owner actually beat him to it). Karl-Friedrich Lenze, fifty-four, applied for a license to open a brothel in Berlin for sexually frustrated dogs. He believes that dogs suffer when they have no outlet for their sexual urges. His brothel would only employ carefully vetted workers of both sexes and there would be a sniffing bar where they could get acquainted. He was planning to charge dog owners $27 for half an hour of happiness.

THE BIRDS

A new phenomenon struck terror into the hearts of the inhabitants of a small Canadian town in a situation scarily reminiscent of Alfred Hitchcock's chilling film *The Birds*. Tens of thousands of crows descended on the town of Woodstock, Ontario, population thirty-five thousand. At one point there were more crows than people—and that's one heck of a lot of crows. With the sky blackened by the vast numbers of crows in the air, and every tree and rooftop and telephone pole home to thousands of the birds, Woodstock was a very weird place to be. But the birds weren't just sitting around. Residents also discovered that the crows were not afraid to attack, swooping down from the treetops and terrorizing them. This mass roost lasted a month, and ornithologists haven't worked out quite why it happened, although the loss of forest to farming land may have had a lot to do with it.

A Canadian dentist came to the aid of a bald eagle left for dead after its beak was shot off. He manufactured a false bill from the acrylic material used for dentures, basing his design on a picture of an eagle in *National Geographic* magazine. It worked so well that his patient, found on Vancouver Island, was soon ripping up food again. Dr. Brian Andrews is a keen woodcarver as well as being a dentist and makes duck decoys as a hobby, so he reckoned an eagle beak would not be much harder to shape than a duck bill, and he was right. A Mark II beak is on the drawing board, since bits of fish do tend to get caught between the false beak and the eagle's skull.

A sweet little duckling had an amazing escape on the island of Guernsey. A nasty predatory seagull had swooped down and carried it off for its supper but lost control of it in mid-air. Now ducklings can't fly, so this one did the only thing it could—plummet. Meanwhile, at ground level, fire officer Tia Farrell had at just that moment stopped to answer a call on her cell phone and sat down on a wall. She noticed a seagull had soared by with something in its beak, then felt a light thud as the duckling dropped on her head and bounced onto the beach, unhurt. Tia took the duckling, which she named Biggles, home for safekeeping, leaving the seagull circling over-head just in case its dinner became available again.

An eighty-year-old man was killed after he angered a group of herring gulls in Anglesey, North Wales. Wilfred Roby had climbed onto a low wall to clean the gulls' droppings from his garage roof using a long stick. His fatal error was to disturb a nest of chicks. The parent birds, joined by other adults, attacked, swooping down at him and knocking him off the wall. He fell, unconscious, and the enraged gulls pecked at his prone body. Mr. Roby suffered a suspected heart attack and was pronounced dead at the scene.

Dead as a dodo, they say, but maybe that will change. Scientists recently announced that they have the capability to use dodo DNA to reconstruct a dodo. The flightless, hapless bird that inhabited the island of Mauritius was killed off by Dutch settlers, despite the fact that no matter how you cooked a dodo it tasted foul. By 1681 the dodos had all gone, but now the bird could be re-created and the phrase "dead as a dodo" will no longer ring true.

A very confused swan living on a boating lake in Hamburg fell for a swan-shaped pedal boat. The male swan would not leave his new love's side and jealously refused to allow anyone near his model bride, furiously chasing off anyone who tried to use it.

Pillars of the Community

RELIGION . . .

Religious fervor leads to some pretty weird behavior. Take Easter in the Philippines, for example. Every year on Good Friday—and this last one was no exception—a few people have themselves nailed to wooden crosses so they can experience the suffering of Christ. They are bound to the cross, too, in a similar way to Jesus, and often choose to wear a crown of thorns. Compared to the original crucifixion of Jesus, it isn't so bad. They usually stay up on the cross for around ten minutes rather than the days that criminals endured in Biblical times. And some of the crucifixees bring their own nails to the ceremony so they don't risk infection.

A group of Christian protestors conveniently forgot the concept of brotherly love preached by Jesus when they disrupted a pagan spring equinox ceremony in California by blasting their car stereos to drown out the songs and chants of three hundred witches and warlocks. Apparently angered by the pagans' joky animal sacrifice involving a chocolate rabbit, the Christians jumped from their cars and approached the pagans; a fight was averted at the last minute.

In most Western countries credit card debt is a significant part of the economy. And do you know who is to blame? Why, Satan himself. At least that's the point of view of Bishop C. Vernie Russell's Mount Carmel Missionary Baptist Church in the state of Virginia. They raised $340,000 from the congregation in fourteen months just to help get randomly chosen members out of debt by having their credit card bills paid off by the church. At the monthly debt liquidation meetings, the churchgoers dance and chant and are encouraged to "stomp the devil" in an attempt, presumably, to stop him causing so much credit card debt. At the time of writing, fifty-nine lucky members of the church had had their debts settled, but also had to cut up their credit cards and go to counseling sessions.

Last year we reported on a fairly stupid standoff between two nutty rabbis in Jerusalem. Now there's been a bit more religious silliness in this most holy of cities. You've got your Ethiopian Orthodox Christian monks and you've got your Egyptian monks of the Coptic Christian Church of Egypt, and it seems that both parties hang out on the roof of the Church of the Holy Sepulchre, which is the site of the burial and resurrection of Jesus, so a holier place more deserving of respect you could not imagine. One of the Egyptian monks sitting on the roof moved his chair into the shade, apparently violating an agreement between the two groups on the allocation of roof space, and an ugly brawl kicked off, resulting in the Ethiopian monks, throwing iron bars and chairs at their Egyptian counterparts. Seven Ethiopians and four Egyptians were injured.

Hallelujah! He is saved! Michael Braithwaite was a porn shop owner in the town of Putney, Kentucky. In Love World, which was brightly painted in red, he sold all manner of sex aids and fetish wear. Then one day God told him it was time to close it down, or at least that is what Mr. Braithwaite experienced, as he underwent a full-scale religious conversion. He piled up $10,000 worth of sex toys, doused them in oil, and torched the lot. And not satisfied with cleaning up his act, Mr. Braithwaite went the whole hog and re-opened his shop as a Bible store, painting it white, dropping the name Love World, and calling it simply Mike's Place. This came as a shock to his regular customers, who would walk in looking for porn and see only God's works. Of course the fact that Mr. Braithwaite was facing an obscenity charge brought against him by the citizens of Putney had nothing at all to do with his miraculous conversion.

The Hindu god Krishna is said to have grown up playing tricks and pranks, but this one was a bit naughty for a god to play. A giant statue of Krishna toppled over in New Delhi, killing one worker and injuring several others. The 108-foot giant image of the Hindu god had been under construction for six years—that's six long years of hard work wiped out in one swift second. Naughty, naughty Krishna.

Giving every impression of a great depth of religious devotion, a South American couple were observed to visit a particular church in Milan every single day for over a month, praying in front of a statue of the Virgin Mary. It turned out that they were recharging their mobile phone from the electrical socket used to light up the statue. In an admirable show of generosity, the priest said that he would not bar the couple from his church and that allowing them to use the electricity was much like giving them a glass of water.

... AND PRIESTS

None of the accidents was an act of God: The Reverend Roland Gray, a Baptist minister from Harvey, Illinois, was sentenced to four and a half years in prison for defrauding insurance companies of over $450,000. His trick was faking car accidents, at least fourteen of them. "I consider myself a man of God," Gray said in court, "but I got a little confused."

Orlando Bethel, a street preacher in Loxley, Alabama, was supposed to be singing at the funeral of his wife's uncle at the Pine Grove Baptist Church. Orlando got up into the pulpit and started screaming that the deceased was "a drunkard," and "a fornicator," and that he was now "burning in hell." Then, adding insult to injury, he informed the rest of the parishioners that they would follow the deceased to that fiery place. Orlando was, not surprisingly, dragged bodily from the pulpit; it was a little ungodly of the parishioners to give him a solid beating and throw him into the street, but they were probably following Old Testament rules (an eye for an eye) rather than New Testament ones (turn the other cheek). Orlando said in his defense that he had been bidden to tell the truth by the Holy Ghost. The truth can hurt, and in this case it hurt Orlando pretty badly.

Catholics the length and breadth of Mexico were appalled when a newspaper published stills taken from a home video. In the video was a priest. Also in the video, his female secretary. And no prizes for guessing what they were up to. They were having sex, of course. Fornicating, to use the appropriate expression. An interesting aspect of this messy saga was that the bishop responsible for the area where the priest lives decided that no punishment was necessary because the video had been made three years earlier and the woman had since moved out of the country. So it's fine to break your vows and betray your profession as long as it takes three years for anyone to find out. At least in Mexico.

In a shocking departure from the typical formula of a supposedly good priest straying from the true path, we have a story of a man believed to be a filthy capitalist sneaking away from his wife to carry out his priestly vocation. Jorge Barange, a Colombian living in Madrid, had been married to Sandra Vega Martínez for five years and they had had a son before she found out what his "business trips" really were. Barange was an ordained priest and was traveling to celebrate mass in places as far away as Rome. Martínez filed for divorce when he left her for good, which is when she made the discovery about his true profession.

This is more like it, though: a very naughty priest indeed. An Oklahoma minister was charged with bank robbery after he held up several banks near his parish and used the church van to escape. Warren Preston Brown, forty-one, a minister at the Bible Baptist Church in the town of Norman, wrote this note (when he should have been writing a sermon): "All the money now. Sixty secs. 100s, 50s, 20s. No talking." It probably had more impact than a sermon, certainly on the cashiers of the Oklahoma Educators Credit Union.

Police in Rome were called to the scene of a violent attack: A tramp was being set upon by four drunken men in the Campo di Fiori, an ancient and beautiful square in the city center. When officers arrived they were astounded to see that the ringleader was a priest. As the police mentioned afterward, there was not much charity shown by God's representative toward a poor homeless man. They tried to calm the situation down, but the priest then led an attack on the officers, leaving them with cuts and bruises before being handcuffed and bundled away in the police car.

Still in the home of Catholicism, a high-class brothel in the Italian city of Verona was raided by the vice squad, and one of its regular customers was found to be a priest from Parma. Apparently he always demanded that his women dress as nuns.

POLITICS . . .

In India, Kamla Jaan is a member of the "Third Sex," but lost her seat as mayor of the central town of Katni when a judge ruled that she was a man, illegally occupying a political position reserved under a quota system for women. Jaan is a eunuch and refers to herself as "she." She was mayor of the town

from January 2000, from which time she was the proverbial new broom, fixing drains, renovating the town bus station and sinking wells, even dismissing the mayor's advisory council. As one of a population of thousands of eunuchs and transvestites, Jaan had stood for election as a woman, but the ruling that she was a man may hasten the establishment of a political party exclusively for eunuchs.

Ever think that politics is a soulless, callous business, populated by self-serving egotists who hunger after power just to deal with their own feelings of inadequacy? Or am I being too cynical? Maybe not, because a Belgian mayor set up a Department of Tenderness to encourage people to be nicer to each other. The mayor of Kruibeke, Antoine Denert, thinks that one of the causes of conflict is the fact that people just don't cuddle enough. He said he would make it his personal responsibility and set an example in his own village by caressing, cuddling, and kissing as many people as he could.

In the wake of the Iraq war, the subject of weapons of mass destruction was raised with Pakistan, whose foreign ministry spokesman, Aziz Ahmand Khan, said that Pakistan didn't believe in any weapon of mass destruction at all; apart, that is, from nuclear weapons.

Transport policy in this day and age is very difficult, at least in the West, where car ownership is still rising. Not so in North Korea, however, where the government has completed a magnificent four-lane highway that runs all the way from the capital, Pyongyang, to the frontier with the evil capitalists of South Korea. Quite why the North Koreans felt the need to splash out on such a massive route, cutting through mountainsides and deep gorges, is a mystery: There is practically no private car ownership in North Korea. The only private cars are those given by the government to famous actors and gold medalists from the Olympic Games. At least the road repair budget won't take a hammering.

In India's Parliament, Finance Minister Jaswant Singh tried to introduce a budget proposal to raise the price of fertilizer, a proposal that would have hurt  farmers suffering from a bad drought. So rather than standing up and making interminable speeches to indefinitely delay the introduction of the proposal, as is common practice, a group of politicians just shouted. And screamed. And howled. For over four hours, until Singh gave in and agreed to withdraw the proposal.

Much as we might like to believe that open democracy is the only way to run a country, some people clearly have a problem with it. Take Romanian factory worker Constantin Simion, from Campineanca. Having lived practically all his life under the dictatorship of President Ceaucescu, he asked for asylum in Iraq (then run by one Saddam Hussein in a less than democratic way). The fifty-two-year-old Simion said that if Iraq refused him asylum he would try for Libya or Cuba—anywhere, in fact, with a totalitarian regime. "I'm sick of democracy," he said.

. . . AND POLITICIANS

The divine right of kings is no longer accepted as a valid mandate for government, but try telling that to the president of Turkmenistan, Saparmurat Niyazov. Big men in charge of small countries do sometimes let power go to their heads, but Niyazov's decrees are pretty spectacular. He's already had several schools, airports, cities, and even a meteor named after him, but his finest moment seems to have been in a five-day purple patch when he made two decrees. First he ordered the names of the days of the week and the months of the year to be changed. (This is not without precedent: Another power-crazed politician, Napoleon, had a go at the French calendar when his revolution was in full swing, but his inventions never stuck.) Niyazov was aiming at names that inspired and uplifted: The name for Tuesday became "Young Day"; Saturday, "Spirituality Day"; and so forth. The names of the months were to commemorate the country's great heroes, starting of course with January, to be called "Turkmenbashi" after his own official name, which means "Head of All Turkmen," while April was to be named after his mother. His second decree was to divide the human lifespan into twelve-year cycles and give a name to each one, from "childhood" through "adolescence," up to "old" (aged over eighty-five).

Lithuanian President Rolandas Paksas lost many people's trust when it was revealed whom he himself trusted in. Paksas, who wooed his voters with stunts like flying a light aircraft under a bridge, declared his faith in a mystic, Lena Lolisvili, for healing and guidance in personal matters. Lolisvili is not any old run-of-the-mill mystic, oh no. She claims that God tells her the future and that he energizes toilet paper, which she then wraps around her patients to heal them. Whether the energized toilet paper wrap treatment works, no one can say for sure, but it is rumored that President Paksas himself was healed by Lolisvili. Don't be concerned, however, that perhaps the president was risking Lithuania's credibility in the international community;

he is adamant that he consults his mystic only on purely personal matters.

In Japan, a local election was won by a professional wrestler, possibly following the example of WWF wrestler Jesse Ventura in Minnesota. The Great Sasuke, as he is known, wears a trademark mask in the ring and vowed to keep his mask on when he is at his seat on the council. "This is my face," he said.

the price of free speech

The town of Virgin, in the state of Utah, likes to be at the cutting edge of politics. A year ago, the Virgin Town Council passed a law requiring all households to own a gun—for self-defense, you understand. More recently, and apparently with no irony intended, in an attempt to prevent "the erosion of the USA's sovereignty," all United Nations activities were banned within the town's borders. (We're not too sure how the sovereignty was being eroded in a place where the UN has no activities.) And to cap it all, in the land of free speech, Mayor Jay Lee announced a $25 charge to residents who want to speak up at local planning meetings.

ECCENTRIC

"Ich bin soooo cool, ja?" Er, nein, Peter, nein. German defense minister Peter Struck paid a visit to German troops on peacekeeping duty in the Balkans. A rock band formed part of the Easter entertainments laid on for the KFOR force, and the sixty-year-old politician leapt onto the stage clad in a Blues Brothers outfit (black suit, black hat, black shades) and belted out a rendition of "Jailhouse Rock" for the boys. When asked how he went down, Struck said later that the soldiers "had mixed feelings."

Do we detect the inability to distinguish between fantasy and reality? And in a politician, does that surprise us? A Norwegian member of parliament was caught playing a war game on his pocket computer, while about him a debate raged about the rights and wrongs of a war with Iraq. Trond Helleland, a member of the ruling Conservative party, was observed on national TV, following which he apologized, saying he had actually been checking his appointments on his PDA when he decided to check out a new game and then got carried away. In his defense, he had turned the sound off.

Commitment and strength of will, that's the example we like to see set by our politicians, such as Felix Arroyo, a Boston city councilman. Mr. Arroyo was so intent on demonstrating his opposition to President Bush's war on Iraq that he announced he would go on a hunger strike. Go, Felix, starve for peace! But it wasn't a hunger strike, it was a fluid-only diet. Oh, well, it's still a significant protest. But then he said he would limit his fluid-only protest to daylight hours, meaning he could probably eat breakfast and dinner. Go, Felix, skip lunch for peace! He then further adjusted his powerful stand for world peace by saying he would deprive himself of vital nutrients only on the second and fourth Fridays of every month. Felix, we stand in awe of your steely will.

We know that politicians can talk until they're blue in the face, and we know that this is just an expression. You don't really go blue in the face—or do you? One US politician did, but not through overuse of his vocal chords; it was overuse of a substance called colloidal silver. Stan Jones, a candidate for the US Senate from Montana, believed (as do most users of colloidal silver) that it would protect him from disease. He started taking it in 1999, convinced that a side effect of the Millennium Bug would be a shortage of antibiotics, little knowing that a side effect of colloidal silver is that it leaves traces of its pigment in the skin. Sure enough, earlier this year, his skin started turning blue-gray; and although he stopped taking the silver, the skin coloring is, unfortunately for Mr. Jones, permanent.

Politicians can't always be expected to be fully up-to-date with policy, can they? Especially not complex issues like unemployment benefits. Washington state Senator Joe Zarelli admitted that he had collected $12,000 in unemployment benefits in 2001 to 2002 but claimed that he "didn't have a clue" that he was supposed to report his senator's salary of $32,000, and that it was the fault of the state offices for not catching him and explaining that he was in the wrong. He reckoned that he was being chased by the Employment Security agency for no other reason than that he was a Republican.

There's nothing like accusations of animal slaughtering to jeopardize your chances of winning an election. The unusual (for a politician) behavior of Makinka Moye, running for city supervisor in San Francisco, was exposed by a local newspaper, following his arrest earlier in the year for bludgeoning and butchering a goat on some waste ground. Unsurprisingly, after the article appeared, Moye was not elected.

LAWYERS

Some lawyers don't seem to have a very firm grasp on reality. Milo J. Altschuler, a lawyer in Connecticut, is a good example, although he certainly had a firm

It must have slipped his mind. The lawyer of a convicted murderer in New York City, Angel Martinez, thirty-six, didn't tell his client when another man confessed to the murder of which Martinez had been convicted. That was four years after he was sentenced. Poor Martinez languished in prison, innocent, for another thirteen years before the facts came to light and he was released, probably with murder of a certain lawyer in mind.

grasp on his client. A federal judge ruled against Altschuler, who claimed that his across-the-knee, bare-buttocks spanking of client Leslie Cerrato in his office was a legitimate trial preparation tactic.

THE WHIP HAND

Before the war in Iraq, as you will all remember, there was a long period during which UN weapons inspectors were searching for Iraqi weapons of mass destruction. One of those highly responsible inspectors was American John McGeorge, a former Secret Service agent appointed as a munitions analyst. Setting aside for a minute the fact that McGeorge does not have any of the specialized degrees that the UN demands of its weapons inspectors (such as bacteriology or biochemistry), there was the little matter of Mr. McGeorge's leisure interests. UN officials admitted that they didn't carry out any background checks on him, which would have revealed that he runs a "pansexual sadomasochistic group." Yes, Mr. McGeorge is a founder of the Leather Leadership Conference, which organizes training sessions for leaders in the fetish community. He was swiftly dubbed a "Saddamasochist" by the US press, but the UN defended the appointment, saying that he had been recommended by the US government (and that he had done nothing illegal).

In a world in which sport is increasingly a serious, tense, money-oriented business, it's nice to be reminded that the tentacles of oddness sometimes weave their way in.

SPORTING STUPIDITY

The US TV channel Fox Entertainment had no idea what they were letting themselves in for when they changed their programming to broadcast a baseball game instead of a motor sport event. Michael Melo of Boston, a NASCAR fan of the deepest dye, was so enraged that the network didn't show him the race he had been waiting to watch that he sat down at his computer and devised a program to send repeat e-mails to the Fox network. Over a few days Fox received over half a million e-mails, forcing them to shut down part of their Web site. Maybe next time they'll warn him. Personally.

A German extreme sports enthusiast claimed a world record after cycling 2.6 miles underwater. Wolfgang Kulov, astride a specially designed lead-framed bike, cycled along the North Sea coastline from Scharbeutz in Germany's northernmost province, Schleswig-Holstein, to the Timmendorf beach in neighboring Ostseebad. Kulov expected his attempt to take him at least eight hours and was amazed when he emerged from the water just over three hours later. The fifty-three-year-old said that a couple of fish came along for the ride, sitting on the handlebars.

Last year we came across the adrenalin-fueled rush that is wheelie-bin racing. This year the sport of potato cannon combat has come to our notice. It's all the rage in Germany, specifically in the state of Baden-Württemberg. Just get a piece of drainpipe, some masking tape, and a can of hairspray to be ignited as a propellant, toss in a few spuds and you have a very effective potato mortar. When a group of truant kids attacked a school with their weapons, potatoes were launched as far as two hundred yards. It's not a blood sport, but it soon could be.

Rugby League is a hard sport, for sure. Wigan's three-quarter, Jamie Ainscough, had a problem with his arm after a match against St. Helen's but toughed it out to play in his next three games before his arm became infected and he was sent to the hospital for an X-ray. The cause of the infection, it turned out, was a tooth embedded in his arm. A short operation later, the tooth was removed and identified as belonging to St. Helen's center Martin Gleeson, who could not then be accused of not playing with enough bite. Ainscough sent the tooth back in the post, according to the Wigan club coach, Stuart Raper. And despite not having Ainscough in the side, Wigan won their next game at Warrington, who put in a toothless display.

Toronto was selected to host the 2002 International Rock Paper Scissors Championships, presented by the World Rock Paper Scissors Society, the governing body of the sport of Rock Paper Scissors (RPS). The world's premier RPS players assembled in Toronto to compete for the Championship Trophy and a total of $2,000 in prize money. The World RPS Society has a strategy to "get RPS used in all households as a fun and safe way to resolve disputes." Pete Lovering beat Moe Asem in a gripping five-set match to win the $1,200 first prize.

In the US, pro wrestling is big business. The WWE (World Wrestling Entertainment) doesn't just script their bouts, they script the "characters" as well (is this sport or soap opera? Sport opera, maybe), two of whom, Billy and Chuck—not their real names, of course—were observed to behave more and more affectionately toward each other on their Thursday night *Smackdown* program on the United Paramount Network. It was then announced that Billy and Chuck were gay, in love, and going to get married. WWE hit the headlines big time, as you can imagine, and the gay media watchdog organization publicly commended the wedding as a welcome break from the usual homophobia of pro wrestling and a good message to the male teenagers who make up a very large part of the WWE's audience. Then Billy (real name, confusingly, Chuck Palumbo) and Chuck (Monty Sopp—a gay name if ever I heard one) announced that they weren't gay at all and there was to be no wedding. WWE, with ratings and profits tumbling, had dreamed it all up as a much needed publicity stunt.

We reported last year on the Extreme Ironing Championships. Well, they've been at it again. The three-man British team from Leicester walked away with the trophy after beating off starch-stiff competition from nine other nations. Challenges at the world championships involved pressing shirts in the middle of a river, up a tree, and while skating on Rollerblades. Points were awarded for creative ironing skills as well as the quality of the creases in the clothing.

An Indian martial arts expert won a place in the Guinness World Records by cracking three concrete blocks in half using his groin, although we're not quite sure which part of his groin he used. Bibhuti Bhushan Nayak, thirty-four, from Delhi, started training his groin after being inspired by a Japanese karate expert. Nayak now plans to break fifty baseball bats over his knee.

can parents get any pushier?

It appears from a recent report that the average age of admission at American tennis, golf, and soccer academies has fallen—to two years old. That's right: American parents are so fired up by the prospect of their kids' earning millions on the pro circuits that they're starting to think that three years old may be an absolute maximum to start training in order to guarantee success. One parent, whose daughter hit seventy tennis balls a day at the age of three, said that with all her daughter's little friends starting coaching at four or five, she feels she has an edge.

ODD

Malagasy (formerly known as Madagascar) has a national soccer league, and the 2001 champions, Stade Olympique de l'Emyrne, even got through to the second round of the African Champions League in 2002, proving they can score goals and win games against decent opposition. So their loss in a league match to newly crowned Malagasy champions Adema was unwelcome. Even more so when you consider that the score was 149–0. Enraged by a refereeing decision that led to a fight between their coach and match officials, the Stade Olympique players repeatedly scored in their own goal for the whole of the match (it works out to a goal every one hundred seconds or so) as the perplexed Adema players looked on. The winning margin is a world record for a national league match.

Here's one for the Stupid Sports Fans scrapbook. Remember, ice is slippery. And streaking at a sports event nowadays is just an unfunny cliché. Unless, of course, it all goes wrong, as it did for a man at an NHL ice-hockey game in Calgary, Canada. Stripped nude and ready to amaze, Tim Hurlbut sprinted out onto the ice before a Calgary Flames game, slipped immediately, hit his head on the ice, and knocked himself out cold (pun intended). Play between the Flames and the Boston Bruins had to be stopped for about six minutes while medical staff attended to the unconscious Hurlbut, and the spectators got a much longer look at him than he may have wanted. Apparently two strangers had offered him $200 to jump over the boards wearing only his red socks, but, weirdly enough, they never came forward with the money. And Hurlbut needed it, to pay the $400 ambulance bill.

FITNESS

A lot of people think keeping fit is weird. I'm not one of them, but there are, even so, aspects of keeping fit that merit a place in this book.

Some people get the weirdest ideas about what is good for them. A Chinese pensioner whose daily exercise routine comprised walking backward around his local lake eventually, of course, fell into said lake, throwing the merits of this particular form of exercise into question. The seventy-two-year-old had to be rescued by some other senior citizens practicing the very sensible and very ancient Chinese art of walking forward. He was taken to a hospital, where he had to have stitches in a head wound.

Sometimes fitness trainers and coaches get accused of being slave-drivers. And the term "being whipped into shape" derives from the same idea—but of course that's just a metaphor. Except in New York (where else?) where the first "Slavercise" class was launched by a dominatrix going by the name of Mistress Victoria. Sadomasochists who want to get fit and get a thrill at the same time flock to Mistress Victoria's classes, where they are subjected to a punishing workout, along with a punishing. Clad in leather and wielding a riding crop, Mistress Victoria expects complete obedience from her group of submissive exercisers, many of whom work out in their S & M gear. The Slavercise weekly classes are full, in addition to which there are one-on-one sessions, and even a Slavercise exercise video for those who want the gain but maybe not the pain of a brisk spanking for getting an exercise wrong or not keeping up.

EXPLODING FOOD

An Italian woman had a shock when an artichoke she was peeling exploded. It gave off sparks, then a flame, eventually exploding in her hands. Police rushed to the home of the fifty-three-year-old woman in Trieste, fearing the dastardly work of a terrorist. No, honestly. Explosive devices had been planted in food products in supermarkets all over the north of Italy for ten years. But tests showed that there were no explosives on the artichoke, pointing to the fact that it was either a natural but very weird phenomenon, or some cunning farmer had produced a self-cooking artichoke that had malfunctioned.

Bet you didn't think there'd be more than one exploding food story. But look what happened in the kitchen of Ann and Geoffrey Britten, a retired couple in Dorset. A bottle of salad dressing exploded in their fridge, blowing the door off and sending it flying into the kitchen door and then smashing through the kitchen window, landing twenty feet down the garden. The Marks and Spencer coconut and lemon-grass dressing was past its sell-by date and had fermented, causing gases to build up inside the bottle until it all went off with a massive bang.

SMOKING FOOD

The smoking ban in New York has thrown up some imaginative ways of getting nicotine into the system. One particular restaurant, Serafina Sandro, produced a menu titled "Tobacco Special," for which the Italian restaurant cooked up such innovative dishes as gnocchi made with tobacco, steak in a tobacco and wine sauce garnished with dried tobacco, and for dessert tobacco panna cotta. There was even the chance to sample a potent glass of tobacco-infused grappa. Chef Sandro Fioriti has more recipes on the drawing board, too, including a lobster and shrimp salad with tobacco. All much tastier than nicotine chewing gum.

DON'T EAT THAT, YOU DON'T KNOW WHERE IT'S BEEN

The things some people eat without batting an eyelid (and it would be nice if we had a story about someone eating bats' eyelids, but as yet we haven't) . . .

Clutching at straws, or chewing on balls? Women in Taiwan have begun to believe that eating mouse testicles will ensure they get pregnant. This new craze comes in the wake of several infertile couples' claiming that after eating dishes containing quantities of the tiny organs they conceived babies. One couple from the south of Taiwan, who had been experiencing fertility problems and had been under the care of doctors, recounted how they were taken to a local restaurant to eat mouse testicles, and after having consumed over thirteen pounds (it is not clear whether that was at one sitting!) conceived a long-awaited baby.

He's not the Flying Dutchman, but he's been eating pigeon food for over a decade, it was reported this year. Gerben Hoeksma, from the town

Doctors in northern India operated on a sixteen-year-old girl who was in the habit of pulling out strands of her hair and eating them (a practice for which the technical term is trichophagia). Although she had been doing this since she was a small child, she had suddenly upped her intake and was starting to complain of abdominal pain. No wonder—surgeons removed a ball of hair from her stomach that weighed over 2.5 pounds.

ODD

of Veendam, has eaten pigeon food for each of his three daily meals for the past eleven years and claims he's never felt fitter. According to Mr. Hoeksma, pigeon food is nutritious, filling, and, of course, cheap. He soaks it overnight and then cooks it the next day until it is soft enough to eat. And, somewhat contentiously, he suggests it may be the solution for famine-ridden Africa. Eat up your pigeon food and leave the politics to the politicians, Mr. Hoeksma.

 A South African woman has had difficulty finding one of her favorite foods after moving to

another part of the country. Nothing unusual there, until you learn that the food in question is sand. Freda Engelbrecht, fifty-three, used to eat half a cup of red sand every day in her home of Gauteng, but since moving to Cape Town she has had to rely on friends bringing sacks of sand back from her home region. Freda says the sand tastes like cocoa (which makes you wonder why she doesn't just eat cocoa, although it's probably not as wonderfully gritty), and despite being diagnosed with an iron deficiency and being prescribed pills to sort it out, Freda still hankers after her lovely red sand. "It's a difficult habit to control," she says.

Cooked lizards are not an uncommon delicacy in some parts of the world, but a Thai farmer has kept himself in good health, it transpired this year, by swallowing *live* ones. Suwan Meunlow, forty-eight, suffered from severe stomach pains as a youth and a kindly neighbor told him that eating a local variety of house lizard would help. Ever since that day, Meunlow has swallowed fifteen of them per day and claims that not only have they kept him pain-free in the stomach department, but they have also boosted his sex drive.

Ms. Shanti Devi, from Bhiwani in Haryana, India, is notable for her bizarre habit of ice eating, which started over fifteen years ago when she was told it would help to cure her stomach aches. She's been crunching away ever since, and now gets through almost 6.5 pounds of ice in winter and over 20 pounds in summer. Ms. Devi, eighty-one, claims that she cannot sleep unless she's had ice to eat. Her doctor advised her to cut down, but she still receives ice from neighbors, who stock it in their refrigerators especially for her.

There's a whole lizard-consumption scene going on out there, and not only among people eating lizards to cure stomach pains. In Nigeria, it was reported that hard-up drug  addicts have turned to the humble lizard to feed their need for stimulation. The trick is this: Collect some lizard droppings (yum!), add some dye powder (to turn it a lovely shade of blue) and a few medicinal herbs (to stop the mixture from killing you?), and liquidize. Drink it down and wait for the buzz, which apparently is the equivalent of that from a shot of whiskey.

Love and Marriage

TROUBLE AND STRIFE

A man in northern India took his wife's telling him to cool his temper far too literally when they had a row about her cooking. He spent the night in a pond and said afterward that he thought it would teach his wife a lesson. The twenty-six-year-old went and slept in a nearby pond so that his absence would worry her and make her learn to cook like his mother. We don't know if his cunning plan worked (although we sincerely doubt it), but he did frighten an early-morning bather, who thought he had stumbled across a corpse.

An Italian man, fearing the worst when his wife disappeared from the nightclub they were at together in Rome, called the police to say he thought she may have been kidnapped. Things moved swiftly after that, as the police immediately circulated her details to all the cabbies working around the night-club. Very soon one of the drivers rang in to say that he had dropped her off at a hotel—with another man. So not quite a kidnap case; more a wife-running-off-with-another-bloke case. Officers arrived at the hotel to find the woman in bed with the man, and when the husband was reunited with her he ended up being arrested for assault when he flew at her in a jealous rage.

A fight between a woman and her estranged husband was played out before an astounded audience of one at 4:30 one freezing morning in Pennsylvania. Debbie DeMarco, a newspaper carrier, was driving along when a Volkswagen screamed past her, driven by a woman and with a half-naked man clinging grimly to the top of the car. DeMarco watched dumbfounded as the woman wrenched the wheel from side to side in an attempt to throw him off the car roof; sparks flew and the car swerved madly before crashing into a concrete barrier. The man, clad only in a T-shirt and socks and literally freezing his n*ts off, fell off the car and summoned up enough energy to attack his wife with a toy car tool dangling from the rearview mirror, puncturing her thigh seventeen times. DeMarco called the police, who arrived and dragged the man off. The man, Michael Becker, told police he had been trying to stop his wife, Lori Ann, from stealing the car from his house. She was charged with, among other things, attempted homi-

Jason Morris must have had a lot of very serious issues with his girlfriend, Samantha Courts, when he attacked her at their home in Horwich, in Greater Manchester, pulling out eighteen of her teeth with a pair of pliers. Police found her with her teeth in a glass, and she then asserted that she had pulled the teeth out herself.

cide, drunken driving, and stalking; he was charged with assault and reckless endangerment. And the car wasn't in such good shape either.

Oh, my, this one is special. And if the consequences hadn't been so tragic, it would have been a scream. Not that there wasn't plenty of screaming in this horrendous fight that took place in the town of Modesto, California. Kelli Pratt, forty-five, attacked her sixty-five-year-old husband, Arthur, after she flew into a rage. Her anger was caused by his refusal to have sex with her, and it boiled over so furiously that she held him down and bit him repeatedly. He managed to grab the phone and call the emergency services, who have a tape of him screaming as she sank her teeth into him again and again. When police officers arrived, she tried to bite them, too. Arthur was taken to the hospital but died shortly afterward: He had been bitten to death by his wife. The local forensic pathologist was sure that Mr. Pratt, who was a diabetic and had a heart condition, died as a result of the bites, partly from blood loss and partly through infection.

Well, this is one way of finding out for sure if your husband is cheating on you. . . . A woman in Indiana was browsing through the weddings page of her local newspaper when she noticed a name she recognized in the list of marriages. It was her husband's. She reported this rather surprising discovery to the police, and he was duly charged with bigamy.

scent of a woman

Enraged that her soon-to-be ex-husband refused to give her half of his estate, Lynda Taylor of Florida took her revenge by wearing perfume that, according to her husband, amounted to attempted murder. Taylor's husband was severely allergic to several chemicals, including perfume, in which Taylor doused not only herself but also her daughter, with the result that simply standing near him amounted to an attempt to cause him serious injury, according to police. She was charged with aggravated battery.

Some men refer to their wives as "the ball and chain," but for Jerry Wayne Thomason, forty-one, of Texas, it was the other way around. He was arrested after a witness contacted police to say that when Jerry and his wife, Patricia, dropped their kids off at school, she had a chain around her neck. The witness had approached Thomason to ask about the chain, whereupon he had given it a tug, saying it was to stop Patricia from running off. When police arrived at their house they found Thomason asleep in his car and his wife in the drive, a twenty-five-foot chain padlocked around her neck. Firefighters had to remove the chain with bolt cutters. Thomason was charged with aggravated assault and unlawful restraint.

NAG, NAG, NAG, THAT'S ALL YOU EVER DO

A Yemeni man ended fifteen years of marital torment by divorcing his wife. The forty-year-old man named Yahya, from the Dhamar province in the south of the country, could no longer bear the sound of his wife's voice. She screamed, she shouted, she argued endlessly, so Yahya ditched her and chose a new wife. Sensibly, he chose a woman who was both deaf and dumb. Apparently she was also "quiet and mild-mannered." Relief, blessed relief.

How much can you hide from your spouse? Della Drimland of Colorado was absolutely seething with rage when she discovered the extent to which she had been taken in by her husband and the reason why. Hubby Bill had for seven years faked being deaf and dumb. Why? Because he couldn't stand her constant nagging. Della filed for divorce.

The Drimlands (above) should have taken a leaf out of the Popas's book. Mr. Popa, a Romanian businessman from Alba Lulia, has been paying his wife $700 a month not to nag him when he comes home from work. He says he is so tired when he gets home from work that he'd rather pay for a nag-free environment, and his wife is happy

SEXY

A forty-year-old prisoner in northern Italy was given a seventy-two-hour conjugal pass by the prison governor for good behavior, and set out to spend some quality time with his wife. Just minutes after their reunion he called the prison and asked if he could be allowed back in. He said that they were arguing and that he couldn't stand being with her for another minute. Within an hour he was happily inside his cell again, safe from his wife.

with the deal, too. Mr. and Mrs. Popa are planning a baby, though, and Mrs. Popa (or Momma Popa, as she will be) will be putting in for a 100 percent pay increase to maintain peace and quiet.

GROUNDS FOR DIVORCE

Reasons for divorce are many and varied, but here's one that probably doesn't come up in court too often. Jean Curtis filed for divorce after she came home to the apartment in Glasgow where she and her husband, Ian, lived, to find him on the sofa wearing nothing more than a blouse and rubber stockings and having sex with a frozen chicken. She kicked him out, despite his protestations that they could still have the chicken for their Sunday dinner.

In true masculine style, a Chinese man got his retaliation in early, filing for divorce four days before he got married. It seems that the man, from the city of Harbin, caught his wife-to-be chatting lustfully online with a cyberlover. And since they had already registered their marriage, calling off the ceremony, which they were still organizing, was not enough—he had to file for divorce.

Avoiding divorce is a worthy thing to do, no matter how shallow and superficial your husband is. Nicole Jones of Bristol insured her face for $200,000, so that if her husband decided she was no longer good-looking enough for him and left her, she would be compensated. Whether she can ever claim on the policy, into which she pays $400 per year, will be down to a jury of ten builders (her husband is a builder) who have to agree that she is no longer attractive. Nicole's husband hated the fact that her figure changed when she was pregnant, hence the desire to have some kind of security in her future as everything moves south.

AFTER THE DIVORCE

Over a four-month period a motorist drove around building sites in California, approaching construction workers in the cities of Fremont, Hayward, Brentwood, and Dublin with the same question: Would they fill his car with concrete? (Apparently, hot asphalt would have been an acceptable alternative.) Finally his wish was granted when a worker in Dublin agreed to his request and duly filled the Volvo to the steering wheel with concrete. The unidentified man said he was trying to get back at his ex-wife. Police were searching for him, even though they conceded that he had not committed any crime.

Here's an absolutely cast-iron, foolproof way of making sure that your ex doesn't get any of the money in an acrimonious divorce. A Swedish man realized the family's total assets (he converted everything into hard cash), then burned it—about $100,000 in paper money! That'll show her.

BEING DUMPED

An Ecuadorian man found that life at home without his wife was unbearable. Pedro Franco Rios, forty, left his home when his wife left him, and moved into his

A Romanian, Sandu Tudose, seventy-four, took it so badly when his wife ran off with a Greek waiter that he himself ran off and hid in a cave, where he promised to spend the rest of his life. His misery was compounded by the fact that she also sold two of his prize bulls and five hectares of land. Friends and relatives tried to persuade him out of the cave, located on his farm in central Romania, but since he had equipped it with a toilet, water tap, and small heater, he was having none of it. He has ordered a coffin for when his time comes to leave the world, and wants his body to stay in the cave with the entrance sealed up.

local cemetery. Mr. Rios's wife left him for his best friend, and he felt unable to stay in their marital home—his heart was dead, he said—so he moved in with the dead, taking with him some bedding and clothing. Now he says he is happy there, and the local authority has taken the view that he does no one any harm and should be allowed to stay there.

LEGAL MANEUVERS

A doctor in Bordeaux was in the age-old position of having a lover who had a husband. He wanted the husband out of the way, so he devised a cunning plan. With the help of some equally corrupt friends, Dr. Jean-Marie Delbosc had the husband, Martial Corlouer, a dentist by trade, certified insane. Several of the doctor's colleagues signed certificates asserting that Corlouer was suffering from acute paranoid delirium evolving toward a major risk of violence, that he was unstable and potentially dangerous. Dr. Delbosc and his lover used these certificates to obtain an order from the local authorities to have Mr. Corlouer forcibly removed to a psychiatric hospital, where he was immediately put into a straitjacket. It took forty-eight days of straitjacketed hell for Corlouer, with the help of an independent expert, to persuade the authorities that the whole thing was a fix and that he wasn't insane at all.

WEIRD

A Romanian woman took advantage of her husband's long-term absence due to work to have him declared legally dead. Stefan Szekesy came home from an eight-year stint of working in Germany and Hungary to the town of Avrig to find his wife, Valerica, living with another man, having notified the authorities of her husband's "death" after just one year. Not only that, she had very conveniently "inherited" his three houses and a car. Stefan was obliged to take legal action to recover his possessions; whether he ever got his wife back, however, we do not know.

COURTING AND DATING

How long can a couple live in sin before they decide it can't go on any longer? Zyness O'Haver, ninety-five, and Sallie Warren, ninety-four, went to an Oklahoma courthouse, where they took their vows, exchanged rings, and the judge pronounced them man and wife . . . after seventy-seven years of living together. Mr. O'Haver, whose grandson Louis was at the wedding, had always joked that he would make an honest woman of Ms. Warren. Let's hope they enjoy a long and happy marriage.

He probably thought it was many years of subtly leading up to the big day, making sure he had plenty of time to weigh up all the pros and cons. She had clearly given up on any changes in the relationship a long, long time ago. So when Peter Morgan of Johannesburg proposed marriage to his girlfriend of eleven years, Susan Venn, she was so deeply shocked that all her hair fell out.

The chat-up king

We wouldn't say this man was silver-tongued, but he certainly had something about him that stuck in the memory of Tina Lange. Tina, thirty-seven, was at a nightclub in Mannheim, Germany, when a man started to chat with her. Tina recalls that she wasn't really that interested in him, but as she was leaving the club he whispered in her ear his desire to see her again—and she felt something drop down her cleavage. Tina assumed it was his telephone number. Later on, when she fished the object out from where it had lodged, she saw that it was the man's false teeth, which had fallen out of his mouth as he was whispering in her ear.

WEDDING WEIRDNESS

Sometimes two people meet and they just click, which is what happened to Stewart Parkes and his fiancée's bit-on-the-side. Stewart's sweetheart,

Christine Browning, his intended, his bride-to-be, was having an affair with one Clint Gordon. Stewart, twenty-eight, found out and arranged to meet him in a pub to sort things out. To cut a long (and weird) story short, Stewart and Clint got on so well at their meeting that they ended up being best mates, and Stewart invited Clint to be his best man at his wedding to Christine. As Stewart said, he and Clint had a lot in common: both builders, both loved football . . . and of course Christine.

Keeping it in the family . . . George Greenhowe of Arbroath, Scotland, married Allison Smith, nineteen, and duly moved in with his new bride and

boyfriend in a coma

Was it meanness? Was it superstition? Or just plain stubbornness? Only the Carasel family of Romania knows the reason why they proceeded with their expensive wedding party despite the fact that the groom couldn't attend. He certainly wouldn't have known, anyway, since he was in the hospital, lying in a coma after a road accident. Still, the show must go on, and the groom's brother stood in for him—what we don't know is whether the bride was partying the night away or watching over her comatose fiancé.

her mother, Pat. The marriage ended after just ten days, following which George and Pat, forty-four, became an item, eventually deciding to get married. Allison, who carried on living in the house during this time, agreed to be the bridesmaid at the wedding of her ex-husband and her mother, at the very registry office where she herself had married him. And she has, apparently, started calling George her stepdad.

Understanding and accepting the many facets of another person's character is key to a good marriage. And where better to start than with yourself? Jennifer Hoes, a Dutch artist, decided to marry herself to show people how much she loves the different sides of her character. She ordered a complete wedding party, wedding dress, and marriage certificate, and told reporters that she wanted to "celebrate with others how much I'm in love with myself." An alderman of the city of Haarlem agreed to officiate at the wedding, although it was not registered in the books. Jennifer ruled out the possibility of divorcing herself, saying that the marriage really was for better or worse.

At least our Singaporean with the paper heart fixation married a real human being (see box on next page). A young woman in India persuaded her father to buy a statue of the god Krishna after

trying far too hard

A sweet gesture of undying love or the manifestation of a deeply obsessive and disturbed character? Nicole Wong, a twenty-four-year-old Singaporean, presented her husband with 99,999 paper hearts on their wedding day because the number nine is associated with lasting love in Chinese folklore. She spent three whole years making them, mainly using folded bus tickets (at least she performed this act of devotion with an eye for economy), enlisted the help of friends to insert the hearts into one thousand bottles, and presented them as a surprise gift to her husband, Derek. He claimed to be touched and very grateful, and not at all scared of the prospect of spending the rest of his life with a potential bunny-boiler.

seeing it in a local shop, then convinced her parents that her life would not be complete unless she married it. The parents eventually acceded to this bizarre request and their darling daughter was married to the statue in a five-hour ceremony. At least there won't be any arguments with the son-in-law.

 It would seem that wedding-day traditions in Bulgaria have taken a turn for the raunchy. In the town of Plovdiv a young couple hired a cameraman to video their wedding day, as you would expect, and to stay with them and record their wedding night, which you might not expect. The video agency thought the request for full-on first-night filming was just a practical joke, but the couple insisted, and had the cameraman follow them around some nightclubs and then into their bedroom. Don't think the cameraman wasn't game, though—he started directing them so that it looked more like a saucy video and less like two non-actors.

LOVE GAMES

Foreplay at the home of Susan Winkler and her husband, Brian, of Green Bay, Wisconsin, went badly wrong one night when Susan forgot that their shotgun (often a key prop in their love games) was loaded and shot her husband in the groin. He ended up in the hospital; she ended up in court on a charge of reckless endangerment.

Here's how not to make a good impression on the person you fancy. John Halliday, twenty, woke up in the night at his home in Stanley, County Durham, to find a leather-clad transvestite standing over him, staring into his face. Alarmed, he leapt up and asked the intruder, who was wearing leather underwear and a blonde, shoulder-length wig, what he was doing. The intruder replied that he was Halliday's best friend and then ran from the house. Halliday spent the rest of the night at his mother's house, but when he returned he found that his admirer had left him a note saying that if he wanted "sex with a trannie . . . he was game." We're not absolutely sure, but we think that maybe the intruder's methods may have put Mr. Halliday off.

Mr. Rosaire Roy had more success in getting close to the object of his desire, though. In Prince Albert (the town, not the piercing), Saskatchewan, Mr. Roy arranged for a "robber" to enter his store while the woman in question was in there and force Mr. Roy to undress. Then the robber bound the two up, thus fulfilling Mr. Roy's fantasy of being tied up naked with her, and setting him along the road to a year in prison.

Telephone sex is safe sex. Usually, that is. But not for the man in Ohio who called up his girlfriend in a moment of heated passion and told her in explicit detail what he wanted to do to her, and how, and with what and so on, for a good twenty minutes, before falling asleep (again, not a problem during phone sex). I know you're thinking it would be funny if it was a wrong number. Well, you're right. It was.

He'd mistakenly dialed the number of his local police chief, who was not amused, and pressed charges.

GET YOUR KICKS

It all started as an original artistic endeavor: Brock Enright of Virginia Beach started filming volunteers

love is blind DAFT

How far would you go to empathize with the person you love? Try this story for size. . . . A Romanian man, Ilie Matei, had a blind girlfriend, Livia Sarlea, who had lost her sight in a fireworks accident. She wanted to break off their engagement because she didn't want to be a burden to him, but Ilie wasn't having any of it. No one could persuade him that the best thing to do would be to dump her. In fact, he went to the other extreme: He begged his brother to punch him in the eyes, hoping that it would cause him to lose his sight, too, and leave him able to understand his girlfriend's situation better. His brother did as he was asked because he was sure that any damage would be temporary. But his punch was so powerful that permanent damage was indeed the result. Ilie was taken to the hospital, but surgeons were unable to save his sight.

being kidnapped in a highly realistic and violent way in order to show on videos in art galleries in New York City. Soon Enright found that he had a ready supply of volunteers desperate for the sexy thrill of being roughly kidnapped, and began to charge $500 for what has been called "fetish terrorism" services. He quickly gained over twenty clients, one of whom was quoted as saying, "I needed to believe that [the kidnapper] was going to kill me." The clients get to keep the videos.

A Thai man was arrested for setting fire to cars, which he did on a regular basis because of the sexual thrills he got when the fire engines and police vehicles arrived. He would torch a car, buy himself a beer, then call the police and wait for the screaming sirens and flashing lights, followed shortly by his own screaming orgasm. The man was arrested when a witness saw him driving away from a burning car. It turned out that he had been in jail already for arson, and on his release had found a job as a volunteer fireman.

We don't usually bother reporting cross-dressing burglars, since, odd as this may sound, there are so many out there that they seem fairly run-of-the-mill in the world of weird-newsgathering. It's always the same: Man or adolescent breaks into a house, puts on a pair of underpants and a bra, and maybe a pair of stockings, and is arrested shortly afterward. However, we felt there was room for this story on the grounds of creative self-expression. Larry Elder, twenty-seven, of Barberton, Ohio, was arrested after breaking into an apartment. Back at the police station he was instructed to put on the standard-issue orange jumpsuit that cell-dwellers have to wear. This was when one of the jailers spotted a sequined waistband poking out from Elder's jeans. A closer look revealed that Elder was wearing, all at once: a pair of sequined panties; red bikini bottoms; a navy blue thong; white lace panties; and four more pairs of underwear, the last of which had a pair of white, lace-topped stockings rolled up inside. That's eight pairs of panties in all. Way to go, Larry!

This is autoerotic asphyxiation without the erotic bit—we think. Students at a high school in New Jersey were warned by officials that a popular practice had to stop. What were those kids up to? The "California Knockout," apparently, in which one student holds his breath until he gets light-headed, then a friend squeezes his neck to make him black out. Those kids sure know how to enjoy themselves.

Old Age, Death, and Dying

OLD FOLKS

This last year the world's oldest person made it to the incredible age of 115. Kamato Hongo missed the celebrations. This was because Kamato doesn't live like ordinary mortals; her routine involves being awake for two days and then sleeping for two days—her birthday being one of her sleep days. Even so, thirty family members visited her house in southern Japan for the birthday party.

When you're old, maybe you forget how as a child you used to play with a magnifying glass to focus the sun's rays to burn holes in paper. That sounds like what happened in the case of an eighty-eight-year-old Dutchman, who was happily reading his newspaper at home with the help of a magnifying glass in bright sunlight. The newspaper caught fire, followed by his clothes, and he ended up in the hospital. So if you need to read with a magnifying glass, it's probably best to do it with the curtains drawn.

Forget what you've heard about banks being callous institutions interested only in financial gain. The ANZ Bank in Australia helped first-time buyer Margaret Cole make the purchase of a lovely little three-bedroom dream cottage in Watanobbi, New South Wales. The mortgage was a fairly standard thirty-year one, which made life a lot easier for Margaret—when she bought the house she was ninety-two years old.

We don't know how many centenarian politicians there are, but there can't be many. And as for someone getting into politics after their one hundredth birthday, that must be a first. Norwegian Ellen Sørmeland, 103, made a bid to win a seat in local elections in her home town of Osen. Ellen wanted to stand up (albeit rather creakily) for young people, and said that she would be able to read all the paperwork necessary for the job, but that her hearing could be better. At the time of writing the elections had not yet been held, so we can't congratulate her on what would be a truly amazing achievement.

Japan is a healthy country, with low levels of heart disease and diabetes, and long life expectancy. A large "gray" population means economic problems as the state struggles to find adequate pensions for everyone. This, in turn, means

what's that, dear?

A seventy-three-year-old German man in Mannheim had a surefire method of getting his wife to shut up. He had an old-fashioned air-raid siren, which he would "crank up and let rip for a few minutes" when he was having trouble getting a word in edgewise. With his wife stunned into silence, he would be able to say what he wanted to say. After complaints from the neighbors, though, police paid a visit to the home of the man and confiscated his prize possession.

more "gray on gray" crime. Here's an example: An eighty-four-year-old woman was at home when a man broke in and robbed her at knifepoint, while telling her, as only old people who are proud of their advanced years do, that he was eighty. The woman tried to hit him with an ashtray—he couldn't have looked that tough, after all—but he still managed to get away with about $600.

DEATH STORIES

LifeGem Memorials, a company based in Elk Grove Village, Illinois, has announced a new way of keeping a good solid memory of your loved ones after they have passed on. They have devised a method to heat people's ashes to 5,400°F, a process in which the carbon converts to graphite, after which they are pressurized into a real diamond. LifeGem's prices start at $4,000 for a quarter-carat.

A British property developer has a very definite wish about how he wants his body to be dealt with after he dies. Robert Blackwood applied to South Africa's Department of Environmental Affairs and Tourism for permission to be fed to great white sharks in the waters off Cape Town. Mr. Blackwood has never been to South Africa, nor ever seen a live shark. And the bad news for Mr. Blackwood was that the authorities turned down his request because it did not have a fixed date. But if it's any consolation, all the experts agreed that if his body were to be thrown into the waters there it would probably be ignored by the sharks and would drop to the ocean floor and be eaten by crayfish instead.

Giving death a helping hand

We don't know if God got sick of seeing Giovanni Greco, sixty-three, constantly making his way to the cemetery of the Sicilian village of Lascari to check on the construction of the tomb that he would one day occupy, but it certainly looks like the Big Guy was a bit irritated and decided that if Greco was so vain about his tomb, he should get a little bit closer to it. Thus on one visit (his last!), he was so keen to get a good view of how things were going that he climbed up onto a wall, from which he slipped, fell, struck his head on a marble step, and rolled into his own grave, dead.

WEIRD DEATHS

The town of Aptos, California, was the scene of a particularly inept piece of getting ready for bed. You know how when your trousers are around your ankles and you're bending down and forward to pull them off, you're in a rather precarious position, in danger of stumbling forward? Well, a forty-seven-year-old man was in just such a wobbly situation right in front of his bedroom window. And yes, he fell forward, trousers wrapped around his ankles, and plunged through the window, landing fatally on his head.

A man who was in the process of robbing a shop in Washington, DC, was put under citizen's arrest by a customer in the shop, who managed to wrestle the robber to the ground. In order to immobilize the robber, one James Thompson, the customer sat on him until the police arrived. Now this public-spirited customer weighed in at nearly 300 pounds, while Thompson, at 150 pounds, was much less bulky. Crushed under the enormous weight of his captor, Thompson stopped breathing and was pronounced dead shortly after the police arrived.

Now I know that those radio-controlled aircraft you see flying over parks are annoying and that the enthusiasts who fly them fall fairly and squarely into the nerd category, but even the geekiest doesn't deserve the fate that befell Roger Wallace. The sixty-year-old was flying his airplane near Tucson, Arizona, when he turned to face the sun and completely lost sight of his plane. The seven-pound plane, with a wingspan of nearly five feet, happened to be heading straight for him at the moment he lost sight of it, and hit him in the chest at full speed, killing him on the spot.

The discovery of this very mysterious death must have been an unsettling experience indeed. Paul Hyde, forty-two, from Barton-on-Humberside in Lincolnshire, celebrated a friend's wedding with a few pints of beer (seven or eight) spread out over a long evening and went home, definitely not drunk, after midnight. The next afternoon his sister and brother-in-law visited and found him in the bathroom, standing up, with his chin resting on a wall cabinet—dead. There were no signs of injury; the pathologist was clear that the amount of alcohol in his body was not fatal; there were no traces of drugs in his system. In fact, the postmortem revealed "no anatomical cause of death." But why was he resting his head on the cabinet? Spooky.

Desperately dumb DIY death: In the Pennsylvania town of Penn Hills, a forty-two-year-old man tried to use a knife to tighten the screws on his granddaughter's crib, after his wife had already assembled it. In spite of his wife's begging him to use an Allen wrench (or maybe, given the male ego, because of), he persisted. Shortly afterward he came running to her, bleeding copiously from a wound in his throat, having fallen onto the knife. Although paramedics got him to the hospital, he died from the wound.

Deadly doo-doo

A mobile phone and an open pit toilet made a deadly combination for one woman in Kenya. As she was using the toilet in the coastal town of Mombasa, she dropped her mobile in it and felt too revolted to retrieve the phone herself. She offered a reward of about $13, well over ten times the average daily wage, to anyone who would fetch it out of the toilet. The first man to try clambered down the ladder leading into the pit and failed to resurface. His friend eventually went down after him—and the reward, presumably—but slipped and fell in, also failing to resurface. A third man bravely descended into the mouth of hell to try to rescue the other two, but succumbed to the hideous fumes and was hauled out unconscious. He was rushed to the hospital but died

The noble and ancient art of angling, craftily coaxing the fish onto your hook, is without doubt a pleasant and fulfilling pastime. But some fishermen cut straight to the chase: They electrocute the fish and scoop them up, saving time and yielding a bigger catch. One Indonesian man was using a homemade device to stun fish in the Mentaya river in Kalimantan by hooking up some electrical cables to his boat's diesel engine and trailing them in the water. But when he stuck his foot in the water—don't ask why, it can only be total stupidity—he electrocuted himself, collapsed into the water, and drowned.

on the way. Even after three deaths the police still had to work hard to prevent a fourth man from climbing down into the pit, at which point the search for the phone was called off.

BREAKING UP IS HARD TO DO

Still with you in spirit . . . Why not stay with dead people if you can't bear to see them go?

In the German city of Stuttgart, a fifty-four-year-old woman who ran a corner shop with her aunt was paid a visit by the police. They had been alerted to the possibility that something strange may have been going on by the fact that the shop was keeping very odd opening hours. On inspection, they discovered a skeleton, not in her closet, but in the bed. The aunt had died eighteen months earlier, and her niece had kept her tucked up in bed while she went about her daily business.

 And also in Germany, in Wiesbaden, a man didn't report the death of his father because he feared being evicted from their apartment. When neighbors complained about the smell, the police arrived, fearing the worst. The corpse of the man's father was still sitting on the couch, minding his own business, quietly decomposing.

SUICIDE STORIES
Success . . .

In Pittsburgh, twenty-nine-year-old Shane Sloan was convicted of killing his mother. She had gotten in the way of his suicide attempt, and he wasn't having that. Ten days later, in the seclusion of his own prison cell, Sloan finished the job.

In the Northumberland town of Milbourne, Boyd Taylor, thirty-six, constructed a guillotine in his own home. Made of a framework of wood and modeled precisely on the guillotines used to behead aristocrats during the French Revolution, Taylor's guillotine measured eight feet by three feet and was stabilized with heavy paving stones. But whereas the French models were operated by executioners grinning evilly, this one was brought up to date: Taylor had fitted it with a timing device that set it off at exactly 3:30 A.M., at which time he was lying beneath the blade on an airbed. Thunk!

Clearly believing he was past his own sell-by date, Emmanuel Gumbi walked into his local supermarket in Richards Bay, South Africa, just as

A group of children playing outside their houses on an estate in a suburb of Cardiff received a shock of horrific proportions when a headless man landed close to where they were playing. A fifty-year-old man had decided to end his life by slipping a wire noose around his neck and hurling himself from the bridge above them. He did such a good job with the noose that when he reached the end of the wire his head and body parted company, his body landing next to the children and his head flying off in a different direction, to be recovered later by police. **WEIRD**

. . . accidental

An overzealous student in Thailand obviously hadn't wised up to the benefits of massive doses of caffeine. The twenty-one-year-old accidentally strangled himself with his belt, which he had looped around a door handle as a device to keep his head from nodding off during a marathon study session.

it was about to close, and marched into the meat department. He switched on the meat-cutting band-saw and put his neck to the blade. Horror-struck staff and shoppers witnessed the blade cut halfway through his neck before he slumped to the floor and died.

. . . and failure

An Italian man from Ascoli Piceno couldn't have been enjoying his holiday in Alba Adriatica. Maybe it was the service at the hotel that made him leap from a hotel balcony in the dead of night (pun intended). Maybe it was the lack of hotel information—the thirty-five-year-old plummeted into a swimming pool he didn't know was there. He was rescued by a passing worker and escaped with minor injuries.

A Romanian man was first of all very unhappy with his life, then almost as unhappy with his hanging rope. Victor Dodoi, forty-five, was planning to complain to consumer authorities about the poor quality of the rope he had bought in order to end his life. Dodoi's relatives found him suspended from a tree in his garden and cut the rope with a knife. What Dodoi found unacceptable was how easy it was to cut the rope, and after his stay in the hospital planned to lodge a formal complaint about it with the Consumer Protection Authority.

. . . and tourism

Switzerland has become the unhappy subject of what is now being referred to as suicide tourism, thanks to the existence of a euthanasia group in Zurich. In a single week, the organization, Dignitas, assisted the deaths of three Britons and two other visitors to the country by providing them with the lethal poison pentobarbitol sodium. Two of the Britons were not suffering from terminal illnesses.

PARENTING

In some cultures, having a girl baby is a poor result. Even so, people generally get over the disappointment and get on with things. But not this Romanian man from Grajduri. When he saw that his wife had given birth to a girl, he tried to bribe the maternity nurses to swap her for a baby boy, which they refused to do. He then tried to get the hospital doctors to supply him with a replacement, but they too denied his request, despite the fact that he refused to take his wife and baby home. He'd always wanted a boy, he complained, and, anyway, girls are more expensive. So the bribe would have been worth it in the long run, then.

In Southfield, Michigan, Tarajee Maynor left her two young kids, three-year-old Adonnis and ten-month-old Acacia, in the car on a blazing summer day while she visited a beauty salon. In the four hours it took her to get her hair done, have a massage, try on a dress, and nip out of the salon for a drink and a snack, her two children died of hyperthermia (heat exposure) in the closed car.

One hot day in July, Jorge Villamar, fifty-nine, of Central Islip, New York, picked up his sixteen-month-old granddaughter, as he had been doing for the past couple of months, drove home and decided to get on with some DIY. An hour and a half later his wife asked him to run an errand, and when he went to his car he realized that the toddler was still strapped into her child seat, baking in temperatures of over 90°F. The child was rushed to the hospital in a hyperthermic coma.

Like, we're really, totally sorry, dudes . . . we couldn't think of what else to give them. Robert and Theresa Dolin, of Crystal Lake, Illinois, pleaded guilty to contributing to the delinquency of their teenage kids by giving them Christmas presents of marijuana bongs.

According to Teresa Milbrandt of Urbana, Ohio, a money-spinning hoax involving her seven-year-old daughter, Hannah, was a "little white lie that got out of control." Milbrandt received more than $10,000 in donations after saying that Hannah had leukemia. Much of the money was raised in special fundraising

Out on the streets of Seattle, Virginia Ramsey was trying to earn herself a bit of money because she needed a few vital necessities to keep her going. She, therefore, sold her baby son, aged four months, for $2,000. After all, the kid had been getting on her nerves, as she later said. Once the cash was in her hands she hit the mall to get those essentials: two Sony PlayStations and a video recorder, and also paid off a traffic ticket.

activities put on by local residents and businesses. She shaved Hannah's head to make it look as though she had undergone chemotherapy and gave her sleeping pills so that she would appear lethargic and listless; and just so that Hannah would be sucked into the lie, she arranged counseling for her to prepare her for her death. Employees at Hannah's school became suspicious, however, when they noticed that her hair didn't look as though it had been falling out, and police were called in to investigate. They then discovered also that a bandage on Hannah's back, supposedly placed over a "port" through which the chemotherapy drugs were fed, covered nothing but healthy skin.

A local newspaper in the town of Rochdale awarded its "Mom of the Year" prize to Karen Buckley, mother of three lovely teenage children.

After the prize had been awarded (and enjoyed, since it involved a ride in a luxury limo to a top restaurant for a gourmet meal), Karen revealed that although the children were indeed hers, she was their father. Karen used to be Tommy, a biker, until she had a sex-change operation three years ago.

Parents of idle teenagers, please do not try this at home. A mother in Cambodia was angry that her thirteen-year-old daughter was out playing instead of at home doing the chores, so she used a logical, if brutal, method of keeping her in the house: she nailed her foot to the floor. The girl managed to free her foot and went to neighbors for help.

CHILD SAFETY . . . NOT!

Darcy Ornelas of Albuquerque, New Mexico, had a few too many drinks at a party and then insisted on driving home, despite advice to the contrary. Ornelas, thirty-one, had her four-year-old son in the car with her, whose seatbelt she didn't fasten (although she did remember to fasten her own). In fact, she didn't appear to remember that he was even in the car, because on the way home in her sporty Nissan 300ZX she got into a race with a Ford Mustang. Repeatedly accelerating and swerving to prevent the dishonor of being passed by the

 Now you know the law: Make sure that what's most precious to you is secure in its seatbelt when you're driving. In Mississauga, Canada, one driver pulled over by police showed clearly what his priorities were. While his nine-year-old son was loose in the back seat, not wearing a seatbelt and jumping around, the driver had a crate of beer snugly belted up in the passenger seat. This exemplary parent received a hefty fine.

Mustang, Ornelas eventually crashed into a telephone pole. She survived, but her son was killed.

Iris Jazmin Rangel of Tucson, Arizona, caused the death of her ten-month-old daughter in a minor car crash. The crash was Ms. Rangel's fault—she simply didn't brake in time. But why was she not paying full attention to the road? She was breast-feeding her daughter at the time.

It was a gloomy Father's Day in Coraopolis, Pennsylvania, when a young man gave his dad a handgun as a present. Unfortunately (or maybe we should say stupidly), the over-eager son had loaded it before wrapping it, and as his father unwrapped the present in front of his son, he shot himself.

TWINS

Jane and Helen Barraclough became the first twins to get identical first-class degrees from Manchester University, both studying biological science. After getting identical A-level results (three A's in physics, chemistry, and biology) and identical GCSE results (eight A's and one A-plus), they went on to study the same degree course. After their identical success, they were planning to go on to the same master's degree and, who knows, maybe even become the first twins to get Ph.D.'s in biological science.

A woman in the Croatian capital of Zagreb gave birth to twins . . . only each child had a different father. The twenty-three-year-old student, who had had sex with two men in very quick succession, gave birth to fraternal twin boys and DNA testing proved that they were from different men. Does this mean the mother will get two sets of childcare payments?

The German city of Nuremberg became a city of nightmares for a while for some young people who were terrorized by a pair of teenage twins. The identical seventeen-year-old boys ran a racket based on the pretense that they were one mysterious person who could be in different places at the

Separated by 11,500 miles, identical twin sisters gave birth to their babies on exactly the same day even though the due dates were one month apart. Amanda Baldwin's baby was due on November 4, at home in Sydney, Australia, while her sister Meagen was due to give birth in early December at her home in Belgium. When Amanda was induced because she was overdue, her sister, on the opposite side of the world, went into labor, about two weeks early, and the two baby cousins were born on the fifteenth. And, of course, it goes without saying that the babies were the same sex—both boys.

BIZARRE

same time, scaring children into giving them money, candy, and other items. Using carefully rehearsed tactics they told their victims that they could run but that they couldn't hide. A typical trick was for one twin to confront a child and force him to run away around the corner, where the terrified child would see apparently the same boy waiting for him. Eventually a child told his parents about the mystery youth who could be in two places at once, and the police were called. The twins faced over two hundred charges at a juvenile court.

KIDS

In the state of Indiana a naughty little boy was sent to his room for eating all the cookies that had been bought for a family party. The twelve-year-old did what so many kids do in these circumstances and ran away from home. What most kids tend not to do in these circumstances, though, is jump on the outside of a train that then hurtles through the country-

Television has a lot to answer for, it's true. But then so does the practice of leaving your gun on top of the fridge and allowing your little boy to watch a soap opera called *Kiss of the Vampire*, in which vampires terrorize a small town. A three-year-old boy in São Paulo, Brazil, shot his sleeping father after telling his mother that if he ever saw one of those scary vampires, he would kill it. During the night the toddler somehow managed to get the gun down from the top of the fridge, point it at his scary vampire father, and pull the trigger. The noise woke his mother, who found herself and the bed drenched in her husband's blood. The bullet went in through his back and then into his left arm, and his condition was not life-threatening. The mother blamed the TV network for putting out dangerous programs.

side at 80 mph. Passengers on the Chicago-bound train spotted the boy clinging to the outside of the train and alerted the conductor. The boy was eventually reunited with his parents, unhurt but more than a little scared.

Left alone in his room in a second-floor apartment in the German town of Korschenbroich, a twenty-month-old baby boy crawled out onto the windowsill, lost his balance, and plunged to the ground. Fortunately for him, he had recently filled his diaper with high-quality natural shock-absorber, and he landed on his backside. The nappy split and splattered, acting in the same way as a car airbag, and dispersed the shock of the impact, leaving the little chap totally unhurt.

A Sicilian man had his family principles tested to the very limits by his five-year-old son. The boy, from Mirabella Imbaccari, took his father's wallet, which contained his recently paid wages of just under $2,000, and tore the notes into shreds. He then threw it all out of the window to be scattered to the winds. Why? The boy's grandfather had told him that money wasn't important.

Amanda Webster called the RAC (the UK equivalent of AAA) when her car mysteriously refused to start after a shopping trip near her home in west London. When Keith Scott, the RAC man arrived, his first diagnosis of a flat battery was wrong, and it wasn't until Amanda remembered that her one-year-old boy, Oscar, had been sucking at the car keys that the astute patrolman put two and two together and looked to see if the radio transponder in the key was still there. It wasn't . . . but it was inside Oscar. Smartly reasoning that the transponder would still work from the toddler's stomach, he got Amanda to hold Oscar as close to the steering column as possible and then turned the key in the ignition. Bingo! The engine roared into life. The transponder was later recovered and restored to the key by Amanda, with no harm to Oscar.

FAMILY TIES

Telephone salesman Al Kinkade was cold-calling people in Riverside County, California, asking for donations to a scouting organization when he noticed that next up on his list was a family who shared his surname. He mentioned this as a means of keeping them talking, and Kellie Kinkade, who took the call, suspected that Al was her husband Dan's long-lost father whom they had been trying to track down for the past seven years. Al had been homeless but had managed to clean up and find employment; now he's found his son, daughter-in-law, and a four-year-old granddaughter.

Just how close can family ties be? When New Zealander Johannes Fransen died while celebrating his seventy-ninth birthday, two days before his granddaughter Rachel was due to get married, the family decided to take him along to the wedding anyway. They parked his coffin in the church during the ceremony, and for the wedding reception the open coffin was set at the end of the hall. Fransen was eventually buried in Hamilton, survived by his wife, twelve children, and fifty-four grandchildren.

STUCK!

It was a little like _The Day of the Triffids_. A woman in Denver, Colorado, found that she was trapped inside her own house because tumbleweeds, some three feet across, had completely filled her back yard and jammed the back door shut. The fire department, which had to come and free her, said there were thousands of tumbleweeds in a pile sixteen feet high. And they were talking to each other, planning to destroy humanity and take over the world . . . not.

A love of books is a wonderful thing. But a Croatian man found that his books didn't return his affection. The wife of the sixty-year-old teacher was in the hospital and phoned neighbors to see if they knew why he hadn't visited her for three days. They went to the couple's apartment, heard muffled groans, and called the police. The man, named as DK, was trapped under a huge pile of books in the bedroom, where he had been for three days. A shelf above the bed had collapsed under the weight of the books, pinning him to the bed and preventing him from moving. The man was treated in his home and did not have to join his wife in the hospital.

A story of immense bravery and strength of character—not to mention strength of stomach. Aron Ralston, twenty-seven, a photographer and mountaineer from Colorado, was mountain-biking in Canyonlands National Park in Utah when a large boulder fell on him, leaving him trapped. After five days he had run out of water and was still completely unable to move, so he used his pocketknife to

SEXY

The worst and most embarrassing adolescent nightmare was realized by eleven-year-old Michael Steiner when he got his fingers well and truly stuck in the condom machine in the bathroom of a cinema in the Austrian town of Braunau. First one of the cinema employees tried to remove his hand, but failed (she was a woman, just to add to the embarrassment) and had to call a doctor, who was also unable to free the boy's prying hand. Finally the fire department was called in and they had to cut the vending machine into pieces before the boy could be released from his condom machine hell.

amputate his right arm, attached a tourniquet from his first-aid kit, and wandered off to find help. He eventually came across two hikers who were able to call for emergency help. (A rescue team had been searching for him for two days without success.) People went back to the boulder to see if they could shift the amputated arm out from underneath it, but the rock was too heavy to move.

MAKING A MESS OF YOUR GENITALS . . .

A man walked somewhat gingerly into the police station in Morrisville, Pennsylvania, with something rather unusual to show bemused officers. He had a firecracker nailed to his penis. Although he said that he had done it to himself, he refused to say why (perhaps he wanted to go off with a bang), and pleaded to be taken to the nearest hospital.

We don't really think about it these days, but the name "laptop" does suggest that you use it on your lap. But beware, gents—here's a cautionary tale to warn you of the dangers of spending too long on that report. A fifty-year-old scientist in Sweden worked for about an hour with his laptop on his lap. When he had finished, despite the fact that he was wearing trousers and underpants (and why wouldn't he be?), he was aware of a certain penetrating warmth where the laptop had been resting. He thought little of it (perhaps it was even rather pleasant—who knows?), but the next day he noticed a lot of redness and irritation on his penis, and by the time he got to the doctor for an examination, it was apparent that quite a bit of damage had been done—he was sporting a painful three-quarter-inch blister that later split and became infected. It took a full week for the scientist's overheated organ to be pain-free and on the mend.

The logic here was a bit cock-eyed, if you'll pardon the pun. . . . In order to prove that he was still being faithful to his estranged wife, a Filipino man cut off his penis. It made some kind of sense, as he told his wife, when he put his penis, wrapped in newspaper, through a window at her house: She could be sure he wasn't seeing another girl—of course he was now in no state to fulfill his marital duties, either. The severed penis was handed over to the police, who kept it in a bottle of embalming fluid while they tried to find the man.

A Kenyan man, who'd clearly got plenty of use out of his genitals, having fathered nine children, took drastic action in order to spite his wife, who he believed was being unfaithful. Ochola Adebe, fifty, wanted to split up with her after they had had a huge fight, so he did the obvious thing, what anyone else in his situation would naturally have done—he cut off his penis and testicles with a knife. Despite very heavy blood loss, he was stable in the hospital.

 A fifty-eight-year-old German man from Düsseldorf (a circus trapeze artist by trade) took a pair of bull castration tongs with him when he

QUIRKY WEIRD Unusual BIZARRE Strange odd

. . . and other people's

Life can be a ball when you set up as a freelance surgeon and advertise your very special services on the Internet—until things go wrong, that is. A Taiwanese man, Shuo Shan Wang, twenty-nine, was convicted in Oak Park, Michigan, of practicing surgery without a license. Wang specialized in castrations, which he carried out on the high-tech bit of kit that was his kitchen table. He was discovered when his last patient, a forty-eight-year-old man, began to bleed uncontrollably while tucking into a slice of post-op pie (not plum pie, we hope) and bursting out laughing. Wang stated that he had carried out fifty castrations; police found two testicles stored in a Tupperware box in Wang's fridge.

confronted the man he believed was having a relationship with his former girlfriend, a belly-dancer at the same circus. Things didn't exactly go with a swing for the trapeze artist, however. He tried to remove his rival's testicles, causing him some fairly serious injuries, but the bigger, stronger factory worker was able to fight back and prevent him from finishing the job, losing blood but nothing else. The trapeze artist was sentenced to seven years' imprisonment and sacked from his job in the circus.

DRUNKENNESS

In the state of New York, an inebriated fifty-five-year-old man drove his car into a ditch. Unharmed, he clambered slowly back up and onto the highway, where he was immediately hit by a car driven by his drunken wife.

An even more chilling warning to stay sober. In Stavropol, Russia, in temperatures of minus 20°F, a drinker was caught short. He stopped in a bus shelter to relieve himself, stood a little too close to the steel side of the shelter while he was peeing, and found that his penis had stuck to the metal. In agony, he was eventually freed by a local man, who poured hot water from a kettle over his member.

Tough love, they call it, and it is pretty tough in Texas. A drunken man was about to get into his car to drive home, in the Texan town of Bastrop, but his best friend remonstrated with him. The drunk was so determined that he was going to drive himself home that his friend stopped him the Texan way, by shooting out the car tires. A fight broke out between them, in the course of which the drunk was accidentally shot to death.

PROBLEMS WITH POINTY THINGS

A twenty-year-old man was fishing in the sea near the port of Chania, Crete, when he accidentally fired his spear gun, shooting himself in the head. He floated in the water for six hours before he was discovered and taken to the hospital with the spear protruding from the top of his skull (it entered through his jaw). After three hours of surgery, the spear was successfully removed, and even better, it had passed through a non-active part of his brain. (Given the stupidity of the accident, that could be anywhere in his brain. Only joking.) So he was back on his feet with no major problems in no time.

 Jorge Hernandez, a construction worker in Santa Clarita, California, had a little accident with a nail gun. Brace yourselves: A misfired nail shot through his eye socket and penetrated his brain. Not only did Hernandez not lose consciousness, he didn't even notice anything had happened until he looked in a mirror. He suffered no ill effects.

And David Lilja, a firefighter in Denver, also met with a little mishap while using his nail gun, which kicked up and shot two 3.5-inch nails—big

Roofing is dangerous work, what with the ever-present risk of falling off the roof. Which is what happened to Wilhelm Mader, working on a house in Reutte, Austria. He lost his grip and slid helplessly down the roof, heading to meet the ground and maybe his maker. His maker, however, was apparently not quite ready to meet him. Wilhelm was working with a friend, who happened to shoot a nail gun into a tile at the precise moment that Wilhelm whizzed by, his foot getting between the nail gun and the tile and being firmly nailed to the roof. Wilhelm was later taken to the hospital after being rescued by firemen with the three-inch nail through his foot and the tile still attached.

nails—into his face. One nail went through his jaw, and the second through his cheek, actually hitting an artery, but the position of the nail stopped the artery from pumping out his life blood. He was quick to make a total recovery.

THINGS IN YOU THAT REALLY SHOULDN'T BE

Keishan Scudder of New Jersey turned up at his cousin's house covered in blood. He'd been beaten up, he said, and robbed. But he didn't know the half of it. Once he was cleaned up, he complained about a very persistent headache and went to the hospital for an X-ray, which revealed a bullet lodged in his head.

A Hampshire, UK, man, Kevin Gilvary, who had returned from a trek in the South American jungle, had what he thought was a mosquito bite on his shoulder. It was a bad one, it seemed, so he put a dressing on it. He was changing the dressing and as he looked at the "bite" in the mirror, a creature began to emerge from it. The yellow head of an inch-long larva wriggled out of the wound before being deftly nabbed and put into a jar. An expert later reckoned it was a botfly.

To err is human. So here are some examples of people showing just how human they can be. . . .

WHOOPS!
Gaffes, faux pas, screw-ups, blunders . . .

Locals had been campaigning for a long, long time for the council to install a pedestrian crossing on the road outside a hospital in Worcester—thirty years, in fact. This year, at long last, the crossing was built, just two months after the hospital closed down.

Stowed away on a ship heading from his native Republic of Georgia to the US, Kheshein Zenbadi was heading for a new life in the land of the free. The ship docked, Zenbadi left his hiding place, and with a cry of "I'm free!" he hurled himself from the ship into the waters of . . . the Suez Canal, where the ship had stopped to refuel. He was taken into custody by Egyptian naval authorities.

Sometimes you can take realism a little too far. A museum in Chester, UK, re-created the smell of a toilet from Roman times, but it was so strong that on a school visit to the museum six of the kids threw up. The museum authorities decided to reduce the whiff factor.

Weird thing number one: Norway had a celebrity moose—Martin. Weird thing number two: When Martin was being transported to Bardu Zoo to mate with Helga (also a moose), he somehow escaped from his van and stumbled sleepily around, having been tranquilized for the journey, until he came up against the all-too-helpful local police who, faced with a dopey moose resting his head on their

Staying with the vomit theme, there was a bit of an expensive mess when a journalist was allowed to fly in a fighter jet to research a story. The Croatian Air Force had specially arranged a flight in a MiG fighter for Kresimir Zabec, a Croatian journo. As the jet swooped through the air at a terrifying 625 mph, Kresimir repaid their kindness by throwing up over sensitive equipment in the cockpit, causing the aircraft to be grounded for seven days while the equipment was taken out and given a thorough clean.

SICK

car, reasoned that he had been hurt in an accident and that the best thing was to put him out of his misery, which, with a rifle, they did.

Now we know that when you entrust your luggage to an airline there is some risk that you will never see it again. But Joe Dabney, of Bakersfield, California, entrusted his wife to American

Airlines, and they lost her. Joe, sixty-three, and his seventy-year-old-wife, Margie, were traveling from Indianapolis back home to Bakersfield, changing planes at Dallas-Fort Worth in Texas. Joe, in a wheelchair because of recent hip surgery, was being wheeled by airline staff to a restroom in the terminal when Margie, who suffers from Alzheimer's disease, disappeared. Staff were well aware that she needed special attention because during the flight she had gotten up from her seat and tried to open the plane door. Despite the fact that she was wearing a special tag, no one was able to locate her, and three hours later, after a gate-by-gate search, she was nowhere to be found in the terminal building. About that time a pilot reported having seen a woman wandering on the tarmac, but a new search failed to find her. Four days later, bloodhounds were brought in to follow Margie's scent. Her trail led to a service road and then stopped, leading searchers to deduce that she had been picked up by a car. There were no further reports and no clues, despite checks on local hospitals, psychiatric wards, truck stops, and morgues. Joe Dabney sued American Airlines for $20 million.

Red faces all around as twenty of Britain's finest and most highly trained military personnel launched a practice attack on La Linea, Spain. Two landing craft were used to take the Royal Marine commandos onto

Motivated, we are sure, by deepest sincerity, Jersey City, New Jersey, organized a tribute on the anniversary of September 11th in honor of the victims. A flock of beautiful white doves was to be released at a ceremony held in the city. And due to deepest penny-pinching, maybe, or deepest idiocy, officials didn't order the doves until the very last minute, by which time no doves were available. So they had to use pigeons, most of which had been reared in cages, and instead of the inspiring and moving sight of a cloud of white doves climbing into the sky, watchers at the ceremony were treated to the farcical spectacle of disoriented, panicking pigeons crashing into office windows, belly-flopping into the crowd, and plummeting into the Hudson River.

the beach, where they swiftly deployed assault rifles and mortars, before two Spanish policemen strolled up and pointed to Gibraltar, a few hundred yards away, where the exercise should have taken place.

A Texas businessman, who was also a church pastor, was jailed after what should have been a run-of-the-mill PowerPoint presentation at a company meeting. What stopped the presentation from being your basic dreary talk was its startling ending. Our businessman tried to open another file to finish off with and the concluding image that shot up onto the screen was that of a naked boy. Things moved quickly after that: He was sacked, he resigned from his position as pastor, and he was jailed on child pornography charges on a bail of $300,000.

 Comedy gaffe: A Dutch charity shop worker sold a disabled man's wheeled walker while he was in the shop. The sixty-nine-year-old man left his walker at the front of the Terre des Hommes shop in Zoetermeer and when he returned to collect it, he found it had been sold to an elderly lady.

Running a secret police operation demands one thing above all else: secrecy. So it was a bit of a screwup on the part of the German police when the criminal suspects whose phone calls they were "secretly" monitoring found out about it because it showed up on their monthly phone bills. Several of the suspects received bills that had charges for a connection to an unknown voice mail number, which was the voice mail the police were using to record their criminal conversations.

In the city of Nottingham, a postman delivered mail to a textile firm for seven whole months before realizing that what he had thought was the company letterbox was actually just a hole in a chimney stack.

This is such a mega-gaffe that we're not sure whether to laugh or cry. A drunken worker accidentally opened the gates of a dam not far from the Albanian capital of Tirana. Much of the city was flooded, hundreds of homes and businesses were ruined, and electricity and drinking water supplies were curtailed. The city was under nearly two feet of water for several days before the flood gradually began to subside. The name of the worker who flooded the city was not released.

If you're going to make a spectacle of yourself, at least do it in the right place; otherwise you lose the point of your protest. As did Jody Mason, who chained himself to the building belonging to the nasty, evil Department of Energy in Olympia, Washington, in order to protest against the war in Iraq, as well as President Bush's foreign policies. Or at least that's what he meant to do. In fact, he chained himself to the building belonging to a nice, friendly, caring organization that helps people in rural areas. That'll show Bush, won't it, Jody? Mason had thrown away the key to the padlock on his chains, so police had to free him with heavy-duty bolt cutters.

It was all going so well. Derek Monnig, thirty-three, and Debra Sweeney, thirty-four, hiked to the top of a snow-covered mountain in Colorado, at which point Derek whipped out a diamond and platinum engagement ring and proposed. It all went downhill (literally) from there when the ring slipped from his fingers as he tried to slip it onto hers and disappeared into a foot of fresh snow. No matter how hard they looked they couldn't find it, even when they returned the next day with a metal detector.

UNUSUAL

A Malaysian man spent a lot of money, time, and effort organizing a very special proposal of marriage to his girlfriend. Lim Sen King, living in Australia, arranged for a giant banner with his proposal on it to be draped on the front of the P. J. Hilton hotel, which was on his girlfriend's regular route into work each day in Petaling Jaya. But wouldn't you know it? On the day that this massive banner was put up, she chose to go into work by a different route and didn't see his marriage proposal. It wasn't until later in the day, when a friend phoned her at work to ask her about it, that she found out. (She accepted, by the way.)

Good fodder for those who like to crow about women being hopeless drivers and parkers of cars can be found in this story from Berlin. A woman tried to park her Peugeot outside an underground station, underestimated her speed (this is putting it mildly), bounced over the curb and a ramp, and plunged down the stairs leading into the Mehringdamm underground station, crashing into a wall inside. Since the driver was neither drunk nor

ODD

Circus performer Jayde Hanson, twenty-three, was showing off his amazing knife-throwing skills on *This Morning*, one of the UK's most popular live daytime TV programs, together with his beautiful assistant, Yana Rodianova, twenty-two (also his girlfriend). In front of a million viewers, Hanson, who holds the world record for the greatest number of knives thrown in sixty seconds, threw a knife that hit Rodianova's head. As blood gushed out, the presenter was heard to scream and the young woman was rushed off the set. Afterward a spokeswoman for the show said it was nothing more than a nick, but another report referred to a gash in her head. Rodianova, who still has the scars from a couple of previous misdirected throws, stopped her knife-throwing role directly afterward to concentrate on her hula-hoop act.

under the influence of drugs (other than female hormones), she was liable to a very manageable $40 fine.

Dozens of mourners had turned up at the funeral of Clifford Smith in Cambridgeshire to be present at his burial and pay tribute to a well-respected man. At the most touching moment, as the coffin was being lowered into the grave, it jammed. The grave had been dug too narrow for the coffin. The family of Mr. Smith claimed that the funeral director tried to "bang the coffin into the grave," hardly the most dignified entry into the earth. The coffin had to be taken back to the chapel while the grave was dug to the correct width.

A thirty-year-old man in the German city of Augsburg was embroiled in a fight with his girl-friend. In his anger, and to make his point, he threw his lederhosen—you know, those leather shorts that we can't quite believe that Germans really wear—out of the window of his apartment. Unfortunately for him and for the city of Augsburg, the lederhosen landed on a tram cable and short-circuited its power, bringing it to a grinding halt on a busy road, gridlocking the city for hours. Police had to retrieve the garment with a crane and made the lederhosen owner pay for the operation.

SORRY, WHAT WAS THAT?

An interesting case has been going on in Ontario, Canada. Back in 1997, Howard Burke was on trial for attempted murder, and the jury was unanimous in finding him guilty. When the judge asked the jury's foreman for his verdict, the foreman cleared his throat just before pronouncing the word "guilty." The

mishearing mishaps

Now here's a chance for you to learn a bit of basic Norwegian. The words "delivered"—*avleveres*—and "killed"—*avlives*—are quite similar. Got that? So too are the words "castrated"—*kastreres*—and "discarded"—*kasseres*. Now if I mention a tomcat and a vet you'll begin to guess at what sort of a mix-up there might have been. A man in Bergen brought in a two-year-old tomcat to the vet, on behalf of his neighbor, for the routine operation of being castrated, then delivered back, but the vet misheard both of the key words. The poor, blameless cat, Enzo, was killed and discarded, not castrated and delivered. The veterinary clinic said afterward that the owner would not have to pay anything.

judge misheard this as "Not guilty," as did the defending and prosecuting lawyers, and Burke was set free. An alert court official caught up with the jury foreman on his way out and established that he had said "guilty," so the judge substituted a guilty verdict and Burke went back into custody. But it wasn't as clear-cut as that; the Supreme Court of Canada ruled this year that it was a mistrial, and Burke walked free.

Plain Stupid

WITLESS WONDERS

What can we say? Is there any hope for the human race?

You'd think that in a gun culture people would be more clued in to the dangers of nasty things like bullets. But no. Robert Covey of Arkansas found a bullet and decided it would be fun to put it on the ground and shoot at it with an air pistol. He hit it on the third shot, and guess what? The bullet went off, sending fragments into Covey's arm and hand. He was treated in the hospital, but only too soon afterward released out into the exciting world of guns again.

Wisconsin is known as the Dairy State, but we think of it as the Scary State when such deep levels of stupidity as this come to light: A twenty-six-year-old man from Madison, the state's capital, was suffering from head lice, and to get rid of them he soaked a towel in rubbing alcohol and wrapped it around his head. Then the stupidity kicked in, as he stuck a cigarette in his mouth and lit it, igniting the alcohol, the towel, and his hair and earning him a long stay in the hospital.

 Texan Kimberly Fennessey injured herself pretty badly, and she only had her own deep, deep stupidity to blame. Kimberly wanted to know whether a .22 caliber pistol worked, so she fired it—not at a tree in the garden, not into the air, but at a frying pan

Selimy Mensah, thirty-nine, of New Jersey, ended up in the hospital with second- and third-degree burns when she started a fire in her second-floor apartment. For some reason (what possible reason could there be, other than extreme stupidity?), according to police, she had tried to open a canister of spray paint with an electric can opener.

she was holding in her hand. The bullet bounced right back and hit her just above the right eye. Mighty fine shootin', Kimberly!

Oh, the levels of irony, the depths of stupidity! James F. Welles, of Florida, is the author of two books: *Understanding Stupidity* and *The Story of Stupidity: A History of Western Idiocy from the Days of Greece to the Present.* They did pretty well: One reviewer said that "James Welles opens a fresh new perspective on human nature." But the writer, offering a depressing old perspective on human nature, was arrested for soliciting sex from a fifteen-year-old girl he met in an online chat room. Sixty-one-year-old Welles spent three weeks corresponding with his teenage friend before arranging a face-to-face date at a fast-food restaurant. "You just have to remember," he wrote in an e-mail to his underage date, "bottom line, I'll be committing a crime." When Welles arrived he was met by his chat-room lover, who turned out to be forty-year-old Detective Todd Dwyer of the Lantana police force.

Police in the California town of Modesto were called to the scene of a nasty injury—a man had had his head split open by a brick in the early hours of the morning. While the man was on his way to the hospital, witnesses were questioned. It turned out that the injury was self-inflicted: The man had been trying to see how high into the air he could throw a brick. And with it being as dark as it would be at 2:30 A.M., he couldn't see the brick on its way down.

A group of Russian train conductors came up with a way of passing the time on the three thousand–mile journey from Novosibirsk to

I know that these days cars have cruise control, but this is ridiculous—and very stupid. Marie Butler, driving on State Road 90 in the state of South Carolina, caused a five-car pileup, sending three people to the hospital when she lost control of her car. What prevented her from being in control while at the wheel was the fact that she was changing her clothes for work. **STUPID**

QUIRKY

An Iranian man gave $1,000 to a helpful man (a real live sorcerer, actually) who, once paid, made him invisible. Confident that no one was now able to see him, the man went straight to a bank in Tehran and started snatching bank notes from people's hands. The problem was that he was not invisible at all (surprised?) and he was soon arrested. Apparently he realized he wasn't invisible when he was caught. So maybe he wasn't that stupid. Police were looking for the sorcerer, too, but he had vanished into thin air.

Vladivostock—smashing their heads against a train window to see who had the strongest forehead. Eventually the pain forced them to stop the train halfway through the trip and they demanded medical attention. But not a psychiatrist.

VICTIMS TOO STUPID TO DESERVE OUR SYMPATHY

Innocent, unworldly, trusting, credulous, optimistic. In a kinder, more inclusive book these words could perhaps be used to describe how some people react to certain situations. But we prefer the term "stupid," or maybe "very stupid." Read on for examples.

In Portugal's Algarve region a silver-tongued and rather pervy man succeeded in persuading four buxom but clearly rather dim women to stand topless at their windows so that they could benefit from state-of-the-art global satellite technology that would give them an at-home mammogram.

There are quite a few ways to get rid of your negative thoughts, and most of them are free. But some people like to pay for things, don't they, because it makes it more valid. Into this category falls Joann Zansky, of Pennsylvania, who met up with a psychic who said she could help Ms. Zansky lose her negative thoughts. What Ms. Zansky, fifty-

A furniture importer was stopped as he returned from Indonesia to the New Zealand city of Auckland because there was a crate of goods that he hadn't declared. The reason for his wanting to keep the contents secret became apparent when Auckland Harbour officers opened the crate. In it were the bones of what the importer genuinely believed was a unicorn. Further examination revealed them to be from a cow or water buffalo, coated with a thin layer of cement to make them look fossilized.

seven, did indisputably lose was $5,400, the pay-ment for three magic wands (stop laughing, they really were magic wands—for the "psychic" anyway) at the bargain price of $1,800 each. Now you may be thinking that Ms. Zansky was not the sharpest tool in the box, but, oh, no—as soon as she suspected that the magic wands were not working effectively, she went straight to the police.

A company in San Antonio, Texas, earned itself a handy $190 million over four years before being stopped in its tracks by a lawsuit. All that money had flooded in from the pockets of hope-lessly gullible people who actually believed that the $40 product that Mark Nutritionals was selling would guarantee weight loss even if the user consumed large amounts of pizza, beer, tacos, and doughnuts.

It's so hard to feel sympathy for a man who injures himself by being a bungee-jumping fool. In fact, the Canadian man who tried to bungee jump from a Vancouver bridge onto the deck of a passing cruise ship was charged with criminal mischief after he mis-calculated and bounced off the ship's tennis court, volleyball net, and a railing before being left dangling in mid-air. William Dean Sullivan suffered head injuries and probably wounded pride, and was rescued by a passing water taxi and turned over immediately to the Vancouver police.

Celebrity is a weird thing. And there are weird ways of achieving it. Many feel that winning a place in the *Guinness World Records* is worth a lot. A fraudster in China took advantage of quite a few deeply idiotic people who were unable to see beyond the limits of their own particular feat. Posing as a representative of the legendary publication, he took cash from a woman who spun on one foot for five days, a man who hung for twenty-five days on a wire stretched across a gorge, a man who swam across an Antarctic bay, and a firm that used the leather from the hides of thirty-eight cows in an attempt to make the world's largest shoe. Still, if it makes them feel any better, they have got a mention in *this* book. . . .

No one likes a smart-ass, least of all rattlesnakes. Matt George, twenty-one, of the state of Washington, was showing off shamelessly for his friends. Matt had a new pet rattlesnake, and to show how cool and fearless and in tune with the rattlesnake vibe he was, he kissed his snake on the lips. His friends told him that he was being stupid and that he should stop; Matt said that he did this sort of thing all the time. At which point the twenty-three-inch rattler struck, biting him on the lip. He was rushed to a hospital in critical condition but came out fine, while the poor snake, which had only been following its instincts, was stamped to death by one of Mr. George's friends.

ABUSING THE EMERGENCY SERVICES

Emergency services in the Norwegian town of Ostfold were mobilized on full alert after receiving reports that an airplane had crashed near a nursing home. Firefighters, police, and ambulances all rushed to the scene of the disaster, expecting to see a smoldering wreck and a planeload of casualties. What they in fact found, after a bit of a search, was a small radio-controlled model airplane.

In the UK Avon and Somerset region, a man called up the emergency services because his wife refused to cook him a meal. He dialed the police emergency line and told them that all she had put out for him were some salmon sandwiches because she was doing some decorating. Not surprisingly, the operator did not then send a carload of officers

A woman dialed 999 in the UK and asked for the police, then began to complain that since she had attacked a policeman the year before, she was now unable to get health insurance. The operator eventually hung up on her.

around, sirens screaming and lights flashing, to make his wife prepare him a nice hot meal.

SHIRKING RESPONSIBILITY

They knew what they *ought* to have done—they just chose to ignore it, and hang the consequences.

A Japanese businessman got into big trouble when he didn't dare admit that he'd missed a meeting because he simply overslept. The twenty-nine-year-old was staying in a hotel in the Shinjuku area of Tokyo, with a meeting the next day in another hotel nearby at 8 A.M. When he overslept and missed the beginning of the meeting, his reaction was not to get to the meeting as fast as possible, make his apologies, and get on with things; oh, no. That would have been too simple, and too embarrassing as well. Instead, he leapt into a taxi and ordered the driver to take him to the town of Koto-ku, an hour's drive away, at a cost of $60. From there, he called the police to say that he had just been abducted by armed robbers. The police assigned ninety officers to the case after the man explained that he had gotten into an argument with a driver who almost ran him over on his way to the meeting, and that subsequently the driver and two other men forced him into the car. They then, he continued, threatened him

A Norwegian football referee came clean about why he rarely gave players red or yellow cards when he was officiating: He hated having to write down the name of a player or fill in the obligatory after-match reports listing the names of offending players. Per Arne Brataas was happier to let players kick each other rather than do his job as a referee because he suffered from dyslexia.

with a knife and robbed him of $900 before dumping him in the town of Koto-ku. In order to help them with the massive manhunt they had organized, police asked the man for more details about his brutal and callous kidnappers, at which point he came clean and admitted the truth. He also apologized for any inconvenience he had caused.

A sense of community, a sense of responsibility, a sense of civic duty: all completely absent from the soul of the man in Olympia, Washington, who saw a dead body in a tree. Quite why there was a corpse forty feet up a tree was and still is a mystery, but the man pretended he'd seen nothing. A year passed, he moved away from the area, then moved back; and lo and behold, when he walked past that same tree, the body was still there. This time he called the police, who went and started the very tricky task of extricating a very decomposed human corpse from the branches of a tree, forty feet up.

There's nothing weird about irresponsible cruelty, but it can be administered in ways that beggar belief. A twenty-five-year-old Texas woman, Chante Mallard, was driving back to her home in Fort Worth after a night out when she hit a homeless man. The man, Gregory Biggs, flipped up over the hood of her car and into the windshield, where he was lodged head-first. Mallard carried on driving the four miles home, parked the car in the garage, and went to bed. Even though Biggs was not dead, not by any means, the most that Mallard did over the next couple of days was to periodically go in to the garage to see him, occasionally apologizing but ignoring his cries for help. Biggs slowly bled to death during that time, when with medical attention he would probably have survived the accident. When he was dead and no longer inconveniencing poor Ms. Mallard with his moans for help, she enlisted the help of friends to dump the body in a park. About six months later she was arrested after a tip-off.

Nutty as a Fruitcake

OBSESSIONS

Just don't ask why these people do these things. Don't even go there. Down that path madness surely lies. Just read the stories and be glad that you have a life.

Ronnie Crossland's main interest in life is cement mixers. Just as some people are avid train-spotters, Ronnie, of Sharlston, West Yorkshire, has been spotting cement mixers for fifteen years. In fact, he took up cement-mixer spotting after deciding that train-spotting was too boring. (We know just what you mean, Ronnie, we really do.) Now the proud possessor of over one thousand pictures of the builders' rotating, churning, labor-saving device, Ronnie has traveled in excess of two hundred thousand miles around Britain and has been overseas, too, armed with two cameras and a pair of binoculars, spotting and photographing the machines he calls "things of incredible beauty."

It was a landmark year for Don Gorske of Wisconsin. Gorske has something of a food obsession and eats very little besides McDonald's Big Macs. He eats two every day without fail, washing them down with Coke, and he actually stuffed away his 19,000th Big Mac this year. Gorske has gone on record as saying that he wouldn't know what to eat if it weren't for Big Macs—shortly before eating Big Mac number 19,000 he had a piece of pizza, but as he pointed out, "It wasn't the same."

How do you dispose of nearly twenty years of your life in a particularly obsessive yet deeply wasteful way? Ask Nova Scotia resident Stanley Jollymore. Now ninety, Mr. Jollymore began pressing

Police, "acting on information received," as they say, raided the house of a forty-year-old man in Costessey, Norfolk. There they discovered the kleptomanic work of a true and very weird obsessive. In every available space were secreted more than four hundred lawnmowers, all stolen. They filled every room of the house and were stacked under tarpaulins in the garden. It will come as little surprise to you, given the strange universe that this man clearly inhabits, that his lawn had not been mown for several weeks.

cigarette tinfoil wrappers into a ball in 1984. The ball now weighs over seventy-seven pounds (he can barely lift it) and at the time of writing consisted of 139,620 carefully pressed wrappers. Mr. Jollymore started collecting the wrappers for a great-nephew who was making a ball, but when the great-nephew tragically had his tinfoil ball stolen, Mr. Jollymore started his own with the wrappers he had stocked up. His technique is fascinating (honest!): Each wrapper is individually heated so the foil lifts off, then the foil rectangle is carefully pressed onto the ball with a rolling pin. In those heady and passionate early days Mr. Jollymore would work at his ball until midnight. These days he tends to restrict himself to just three or four hours a day. He's not really sure quite why he does it (we know why: he's an obsessive), but he plans to stop when he's amassed 140,000 wrappers.

When Tony Alleyne's wife walked out on him a few years ago, he was, naturally, devastated. Thank heavens he had his Star Trek obsession to get him through the dark times (maybe it was why she left in the first place . . .). He set about transforming the interior of his apartment into the interior of the Starship Enterprise. Now that it's finished, the apartment, in Hinckley, Leicestershire, has a gigantic warp core-drive (which alone took two years to construct),

a life-size transporter control (beam me up, Tony), an infinity mirror, voice-activated lighting, and much more. Anything that moves, like the doors, does so to the accompaniment of an authentic swish, beep, or electronic chirp. Alleyne ditched the cooker and washing machine because they didn't look right as the flat developed, and the windows have been blacked out so that the outside world doesn't intrude. After ten years and tens of thousands of dollars and working seven days a week, Alleyne put his Star Trek apartment up for sale on eBay, starting price $2 million. Therapy complete.

NUTTY ACHIEVEMENTS

You probably didn't know that there was a record for standing naked in subzero conditions, much less that someone has now broken that record. Jin Songhao, forty-eight, from China's Heilonjiang province, broke his own record of three hours and forty-six minutes, which he set in 2000 by going to what was described as a "scenic spot" where the temperature had plunged to -20°F and standing there naked for four hours.

An Indian, Farhat Khan, from the town of Bhopal, has a special talent, or so he believes. Khan has claimed a place in the record books for being the fastest typist to use one finger. He can type sixty words per minute (a very respectable speed for any typist) in either Hindi or English, using just one finger. He says that what other people do using both hands, he can do with one finger. Or as we say, what he does completely pointlessly with one finger, other people do perfectly happily with both hands. Anyway, his son is very proud of him.

INHABITANTS OF PLANET WEIRD

Twenty-one-year-old Michael Marcum of Missouri was found guilty of stealing 350 pounds of electrical transformers from a power company, the idea being

In Lincolnshire, a woman was admitted to a hospital when she claimed that she wasn't quite herself. In fact she believed that she was the singer Barry Manilow, and when she was taken into the hospital she was carrying several of Mr. Manilow's wonderful records. The police description of the sixty-year-old woman included the line "shrill voice"—perhaps she is Barry after all.

to build a time machine so that he could travel into the future, find out the winning lottery numbers, and then travel back to buy his tickets.

Probably the richest inhabitant of the Planet Weird, this one. Over an amazingly short (some would say suspiciously short) period of time, forty-four-year-old Andrew Carlssin made his fortune on Wall Street. Starting with an $800 stake, Carlssin took a mere two weeks to build up a portfolio valued at over $350 million, every trade he made soaring due to unexpected developments in business. The Securities and Exchange Commission was as suspicious as you or I would be, and he was led away in handcuffs at the end of January 2003, accused of insider dealing. When the questioning started, however, Carlssin took his interrogators by surprise with a four-hour confession based on the fact that he was a time traveler who had come back from two hundred years in the future (2256, to be precise), which was how he knew exactly where to make his investments. In return for lenient treatment and being allowed to return to his "time craft," Carlssin offered to say where Osama bin Laden could be found and what the cure for AIDS was. He refused to reveal the location of his time machine or explain how it works for fear the technology would fall into the wrong hands. Although officials are confident that Carlssin is making up his stories, the slightly uncanny aspect of this affair is that there is no record of an Andrew Carlssin existing anywhere before this Andrew Carlssin turned up—as an adult—in December 2002.

Planet Paranoia, in the same solar system as Planet Weird, is where Benny Zavala is from, although he now lives in the town of Oxnard, California. Zavala dissected his pet guinea pig because he thought the government had planted a camera in its head to spy on him. Zavala was convicted of animal cruelty and released on bail. A neighbor had contacted police after Zavala ripped open the animal's head, convinced also that its teeth were bar-coded. Shortly afterward he telephoned relatives to tell them that the guinea pig was dead.

It's amazing what governments will sneakily put inside your head—if your head is ready for it, that is. American Brian J. Samdahl, forty-one, was charged with stabbing a stranger fifteen times at a Wal-Mart in Illinois. He told the police in all earnestness what the problem was: His government-implanted computer chip was malfunctioning.

In the state of Alabama, a man was charged with possession of marijuana and told the arresting officers that he supposed God had informed on him. Why? Because he had been rolling his joints with pages torn from a Bible. His name? Jesus Santana.

Scott Caruthers, fifty-seven, was arrested in the state of Maryland, charged with the attempted murder of two men. The men were both ex-husbands of two of Caruthers's "disciples" (Caruthers was the leader of a cult, so of course he had disciples). And, of course, as he told police, he was also an alien who reported back to the mother ship by giving messages to cats.

Were they dreaming or was it real? Police in Honolulu, Hawaii, had to pinch themselves when they were called out to investigate bizarre reports of a body floating down a river toward

In Cambodia, Dem Mam, fifty-four, the leader of a fringe Buddhist cult, was let off the hook after three of his disciples followed his teachings and set themselves on fire in a bath of gasoline. Dem Mam had told them that ritual suicide was the only path to heaven, but when police questioned him about the three suicides, he explained that he himself didn't need to do this because he was already holy enough.

Honolulu Harbor. Sure enough, there was the motionless body of a woman floating serenely along with the current. When the officers tried to drag her from the water, though, she woke up with a shriek. The thirty-seven-year-old local woman said only that she had been fast asleep and dreaming when the officers pulled her out and that she had not the faintest idea how she had ended up floating down the river.

Work and Business Life

COMMERCE

Profit isn't a dirty word, especially in that newly born sector of America's incredibly diverse service industry—professional pooper scooping. That's right: Why bother cleaning up your dog's mess when you can employ cheery, smartly uniformed professionals to do it? California, unsurprisingly, has the greatest concentration of animal waste removal services, with appropriately pun-tastic names. You can call up Scoopity Doo Dog, Scoop Doggy Doo, Doody Dude, or The Weekly Scoop, while ScoopMasters uses the attractive slogan: "If your dog can poop it . . . we can scoop it."

When you're not selling enough carrots, the answer is obvious: scratch cards with topless women on them. Not the obvious marketing solution? Well, Ricardo Monteavaro, a Chilean greengrocer from Santiago, launched the scratch cards at his shop and gave a card away with each pack of "ready-to-eat" carrots, a newly launched product. The little panel that you scratch off is located on the woman's breasts, and winning cards pay $20 plus the sight of the hidden nipples. And if that wasn't enough, the winning card will also double as a calendar. Do you think this just might be aimed at men?

It doesn't pay to make assumptions about whom your clients may or may not be. You never know who might want your product after all, so advertise to everyone. That seems to be the case in the Minnesota town of Stewartsville, where Pure Pleasure (a sex shop) sits alongside the Midwest Baptist Church. The owner of Pure Pleasure put out a double-sided advertising board especially for the churchgoers to read (hey, if they're churchgoers then they might also be . . . goers). On one side of the board, which you see as you drive toward the church, is printed, "And God said go out into the world and have great sex. God's gift to women. Amen and amen." On the other side, visible as you leave the church, it reads, "No need to mail order. Gay videos in stock. Clergy discount. Have good sex. Hallelujah!" Apparently the congregation at the Midwestern Baptist Church were not amused; nor has the Reverend Joseph Grimaldi been in for his clergy discount (as far as we know).

The Dutch have a reputation for tolerance, and in a country where, according to statistics, 48 percent of the population is overweight, there may be a need for it. Last summer a Dutch businessman hit on a way of demonstrating this celebrated tolerance and making good money at the same time: special vacations for fat people. Juriaan Klink built a special 112-room hotel in Mexico with extra-large rooms, doors, beds, and chairs. And travel operator Frank Mimpen is running the vacations to the Hotel Freedom Paradise without making the prices extra-large—the bulky customers only have to pay extra if they want bigger seats on the flight out.

value for money

A single fruit was bought for over $80,000 in China. The lychee, once the favorite delicacy of emperors, came from a highly prized four-hundred-year-old tree in Zengcheng and was bought at auction by the owner of a clothes export business for a family banquet at which the lychee would be eaten. The price—of $86,000, to be precise—dwarfed the amount paid for the most expensive lychee last year, a mere $10,000; and the rest of this year's crop, comprising nine more lychees, raised $120,000.

WORKING LIFE

A much praised young British writer (no, not me) decided to quit the world of literature because his work was making him too fat. Thirty-year-old Dan Rhodes had been named by Granta, a literary magazine, in its list of Best Young British Novelists, but his approach to his work was putting too much of a strain on his body. Rhodes's typical writing day would include the consumption of eight cans of premium lager to keep his literary juices flowing. And since finishing his acclaimed first novel (and easing up on the booze) he has lost thirty pounds in weight.

Ian Jewell must have been an experienced skinflint—one of those people who share their cranky money-saving techniques on the Internet—and he impressed his bosses, too. Mr. Jewell, a council chief on the West Somerset District Council, discovered that the toilet paper supplied to the council for use in public and council toilets did not have the stipulated 320 sheets per roll. His eagle-eyed counting skills certainly wiped the grins off the suppliers' faces as they ended up having to pay $35,000 in compensation for supplying 200-sheet rolls. Flushed with the success of the court case, Jewell's bosses were debating how best to reward him.

It's a tough job, but someone has to do it. Hideo Tsuda has become Japan's leading manufacturer of pubic wigs. He started off making toupées, but one day a customer mentioned that his teenage daughter was worried that she was a little sparse down there and asked Hideo if he could help to cover her embarrassment. Hideo obliged with his first-ever pubic wig. With total sales now topping the five thousand mark, his client base has expanded to include older men who want dark pubic wigs that make them appear younger when they visit hot springs, where the Japanese bathe naked.

CORPORATE MADNESS

Last year we found workers being trained by flying Elvises. This year we discovered a report about the United States Postal Service wisely investing millions of taxpayers' dollars to send their executives on team-building conferences that involved exercises in wrapping each other in tinfoil and toilet paper, building sand castles in freezing cold weather, and making animal noises, not to mention dressing in cat costumes and asking pretend wizards for advice.

Two firms in New Zealand resorted to a rather primitive but very effective way of settling a legal dispute. Telecom's firm TeamTalk was in dispute with radio communications company MCS about accessing its network. As a lengthy, time-consuming, and potentially very expensive court case loomed, the boss of TeamTalk opted for the swift, manly way of settling things. He challenged MCS boss Allan Cosford to an arm-wrestling match. Cosford accepted the challenge, and the best-of-three contest was held in an Auckland gym. With over $130,000 at stake, muscles were flexed and the two men got down to it, with the MCS chief emerging the victor. David Ware admitted that it hurt to lose, but it was less painful than dealing with lawyers.

In Bradford, consultants were paid $40,000 to come up with an appropriate name for the result of the merging of the university and another college in the city. What did those highly paid clever consultants come up with? Their suggestions were: Bradford University, University of Bradford, and, wait for it, The University of Bradford. Money well spent?

Reverse psychology, it's called, and it certainly fooled the employment market in Sweden when a social worker tried a somewhat alternative approach to job-hunting after several unsuccessful attempts. "I want a well-paid job. I have no imagination, I am antisocial, uncreative, and untalented," was Angelika Wedberg's advertisement in a Gothenburg newspaper. Within a couple of days she was swamped with job offers (although we don't know what sort of jobs they were . . .).

DREAM CAREERS

It's a pain having to get all those stupid qualifications that you usually seem to need for your dream job. Some people just don't bother and plow ahead, assuming that practice makes perfect and it's enthusiasm that really counts.

The death of Joseph Anthony Giannini, fifty-three, in Washington, DC, changed everyone's view of him somewhat. He had been well known among friends, neighbors, and colleagues as a retired cop of the most fearsome variety, always with a story to tell about how tough it was out there on the streets. The cab of his truck was full of mementos from his squad-car days—a siren, flashing lights, ticket books; he had several police badges, ID cards, and police academy diplomas, and was a proud member of a society restricted to officers and ex-officers, the Fraternal Order of Police. Police investigated his death because it was from a gunshot wound, and it turned that all his memorabilia were either falsified or didn't belong to him, since no record existed of Giannini's ever having been a cop. What the records did show was that Giannini had once been arrested for impersonating a police officer.

Egyptian police arrested a man who, despite not having received anything more than a primary school education, carried out brain surgery on a number of people. Armed with a forged secondary school certificate and claiming to have studied brain surgery in Cairo and in Germany, the forty-year-old saw about two hundred patients a week in the oasis town of Fayoum, near Cairo. He operated on many of his patients, charging a very reasonable twenty-two Egyptian pounds (about $5) each. The fate of those who entrusted their brains to him is not known.

It must have been fun while it lasted—and it lasted twenty-two years. Five women, including a former primary school teacher and a waitress, ran a doctors' surgery in Binningham, Switzerland, prescribing pills, carrying out checkups, and even conducting cancer tests. One patient discovered that her "doctor" had no medical training and reported the practice to the authorities. Spoilsport.

Another medical charlatan of a very weird nature was arrested for his unfounded claims. A holy man, Garoju Kanakachari, in the town of Vijayawada, in India, claimed he had the power to cure disease by gazing into the patient's eyes. After complaints were lodged against him, police took him to a hospital to demonstrate his magical ability. He was asked to deal with a patient who had a fever; Kanakachari did his thing, staring into the patient's eyes, and then the doctors took the man's temperature. It had gone up.

PAYMENT IN KIND

Money makes the world go round, but sometimes you have to be creative when it's in short supply.

A Serbian holiday spa changed its payment policy and suddenly all 220 rooms were fully booked. Managers at the Vrujci spa complex, sixty miles south of Belgrade, told guests they could pay in goods if they didn't have enough money, and that they would take anything from eggs to car parts in preference to letting rooms stay empty. So a company from Ljubovija paid for their workers' holiday in coffins. Fifty of them, to be precise. The enterprising spa director, Ljubisa Maric, soon managed to sell them on to an undertaker.

Getting a ticket for an Elton John concert is not easy, but Canadian Brandy Elliott managed to get herself two tickets to see Elton's Saskatchewan show thanks to a competition on her local radio station. A pair of tickets to the sell-out show (it sold out in just ninety minutes) was offered to the person who could collect the most grasshoppers! And sure enough, driving a truck with netting attached through fields and ditches, Brandy collected thirty-nine thousand of the pesky insects. After a weekend's work collecting she took them to the radio station for the official count and discovered that she had won by a mere six thousand grasshoppers. And that she and the other competitors had all done the local farmers a big favor.

Uttar Pradesh Agro, an Indian agricultural company, was in debt to the state's Cow Welfare Commission to the tune of $125,000—a sum it could not afford to pay back when the end of the loan term arrived. The company offered a solution, though: to repay the debt in earthworms. The Cow Welfare Commission accepted and two gigantic consignments of worms were sent to two of the commission's maintenance centers to be used in "vermiculture composting."

In the Bulgarian town of Panicino, a local company went bankrupt and was forced to lay off every one of its 603 employees, and in that far-from-lively economic climate, there was no money left to pay them off with. The administrators of the bankruptcy used the only assets available to them to reward the workers—the company's product. Combs. At the time of writing, thirty-two thousand combs had been given out to the employees (we work that out at about fifty-three combs per head, pun intended) at a value of fifty cents per comb.

Kathryn Smith, twenty-one, of Enid, Oklahoma, offered her seven-month-old daughter to a neighbor in exchange for a Chihuahua puppy the woman had for sale at $200. Smith was charged with trafficking in children.

In most of Europe, the top soccer players move clubs for unbelievable transfer fees. In Norway, though, which doesn't have the economic power of other countries, things are different. Third Division side Vindbjart sold striker Kenneth Kristensen to rival side Flekkerøy for his weight in prawns. Fresh prawns, that is, not frozen. Kristensen spent the off-season not watching his weight too carefully, apparently.

Science and Technology

QUIRKY WEIRD
Unusual BIZARRE
Strange odd

INVENTIONS

Dominic Skinner, from Surrey, came up with a great boon to the dedicated drinker–dunker. If you can't bear to have a cup of tea or coffee without an accompanying cookie or two, and your pleasure is to dip your cookie, you've got to get ahold of one of these: a mug with a cookie shelf built into the base, so that the drinker has one hand free while drinking. The slot in the bottom of the mug is big enough to hold three cookies, and the mug has left-handed and right-handed versions that keep the opening facing away from the drinker so the cookies don't fall out when the user drinks.

An invention came out of Japan that claimed to translate dog noises into human expressions. The English-language version was all set to hit the US with its sixty-seven million or so dogs at $120; it's a small wireless microphone that affixes to the dog's collar to pick up every woof, yelp, and whine the pooch makes. The microphone transmits the sounds to a palm-sized console, which then displays a phrase that expresses the dog's mood. The gadget was developed with the help of acoustics experts and animal psychologists . . . and it's called Bowlingual.

The ultimate in discretion could be a handsome (and not cheap, at about $1,500) bookcase that will convert into your very own coffin when you shuffle off this mortal coil. Dutch designer Hans Rademaker thought of the bookcase as an art student and finally turned the idea into reality this year. The bookcase has seven shelves that are made so that they can be moved and fitted together to make the coffin lid. And maybe you can be buried with a few of your favorite books from the bookcase, too.

A British designer made what could be a godsend for the struggling Church of England— the world's first inflatable church, a forty-seven-foot-high plastic wonder, complete with a blow-up organ, pulpit, altar, Gothic arches, and fake stained-glass windows. According to designer Michael Gill, his inflatable church could be carried around by vicars in the back of a van and set up anywhere (in city parks or in town squares, for example) for impromptu church services to boost dwindling attendances. Gill has had inquiries about his invention from Belgium, South Korea, and the US, and has written to the pope to see if the Vatican is interested in buying one. Imagine, an inflatable St. Peter's. And if his blow-up church is a success, Gill plans to diversify into pubs and nightclubs.

CLOTHING INNOVATIONS

Last year we brought you news of a shirt that rolled up its own sleeves and hemorrhoid-curing underwear. Let's see what barely believable additions to the world's wardrobe there were this year.

UK bra manufacturer Triumph has the bra for the way you are. Their Hong Kong branch designed the bra for the way you want to be, as long as you want to be moist. They came up with an aloe vera bra and underwear set that continually moisturizes and lubricates the skin for up to forty washings.

And if you suffer **BIZARRE** when it's your time of the month, ladies, then look no further than B. L. Korea Co.'s menstrual pain-reducing pants. It would appear that they contain substances that cut pain and improve circulation. And your guarantee of safety is that these substances were approved by the Korean Institute of Construction Materials. Phew.

Still in the Far East, where the concept of life-enhancing clothing is a vibrant one, we have the "Ki" business suit from Cheil Industries. The hardworking executive who dons one of these marvels will, according to the theory, be protected from electromagnetic radiation emitted by computer and TV screens, and given an energy boost. The secret lies in the sachets of powdered charcoal and jade sewn into the suit's crotch and armpits. Don't laugh, they've been selling really well.

 Staying with the underwear theme, how about a pair of ready-soiled boxer shorts? Not in that sense, though. For the very reasonable sum of $12, you can get a pair of boxers that is infused with granules of yellow soil that are supposed to emit far-infrared rays to reduce odor and improve circulation (of blood, not the odor). These wonder-undies are manufactured by, believe it or not, Kolon Corporation. And the inventor responsible for them, a Mr. Kwon, has also blessed the Korean nation with the invention of the incredible "Vitamin D slacks." Whatever next?

Serbian inventor Slavomir Adamovic came up with a real gem and struck a blow in the battle against office sexual harassment: women's pants that have a microchip alarm embedded in the rear. The microchip is touch-sensitive and causes a high-pitched beep to sound whenever the wearer has her bottom pinched. The inventor's aim is to render every office where women's bottoms suffer at the pinching hands of their male colleagues a safer place. We can't help wondering what happens when the wearer sits down, presumably emitting a beep, but we just might find out soon because an Italian company has shown an interest in developing the product.

Australian scientists have invented a bra that will come in very handy for women who get embarrassed running for the bus, for example, when there's a little too much bounce going on. This "smart bra," invented by scientists at Wollongong, is made from a fabric that contracts when there is extra strain on it. It actually tightens its own straps, adding extra support when it's needed.

ACADEMIC RESEARCH

Fresh from a Ph.D. in the Blindingly Obvious, Canadian psychologist Michel Lariviere produced a paper for the Correctional Services of Canada in which he suggested, with great insight, that most prison guards don't respect the inmates. And that's a problem.

In the state of New York, the University of Buffalo spent $4 million on a study carried out by its Research Institute on Addictions, which revealed that employees are much more likely to call in sick if they have drunk alcohol the night before. Those employees could probably have told them that for free.

Those clever people at the Harvard School of Public Health commissioned a survey that found that people report more noise and other disruptions in binge-drinking college neighborhoods than in other neighborhoods. Would you believe it?

Researchers at Iowa State University brought out a study that demonstrated that TV viewers had more difficulty paying attention to the commercials during programs containing explicit sex than other types of program. Advertisers, take note.

A group of scientists at the National Physical Laboratory have developed superblack—a black that is blacker than your everyday black. Just how black is it? It's fifty times blacker than the blackest color a newspaper can print, that's how black it is. It's blacker than the blackest paint a specialist paint manufacturer can produce, that's how black it is. Also, superblack absorbs 99.7 percent of light, which means almost no light is reflected from the surface. It has been designed for scientific applications, but artists have expressed an interest. Wealthy artists, we assume, since it costs $1,000 for enough to cover two square inches, or $60,000 for a square foot.

CYBERDEATH

South Korea is one of the most Internet-wired, computer-mad countries on earth, so many people spend a lot of time and energy on gaming. But an eighty-six-hour computer-game marathon proved too much for one twenty-four-year-old. Nearly four days

after sitting down at a computer in an Internet café in Kwangju, the man, who had had almost no sleep or food, collapsed, then revived just enough to make it to the toilet, where he collapsed again and died.

In Taiwan, they haven't got the same stamina in front of the screen, apparently. A twenty-seven-year-old man died after a mere thirty-two hours of video games. Lien Wen-cheng was found foaming at the mouth and bleeding from his nose on the floor of a cyber café's toilet and died despite being rushed to a hospital in the town of Fengyuan. It is thought that Lien died of exhaustion due to having sat in the same position for too long.

TECHNOSTALKER

Paul Seidler, a resident of the state of Wisconsin, got a global positioning system (GPS) and secretly fitted it under the hood of the car belonging to the woman he was stalking. Then, no matter where poor Connie Adams went, the creepy Seidler would turn up as if he, rather than his GPS, could read her mind.

BOTCHED OPERATIONS

Teri-Lynn Tibbo of Nova Scotia, Canada, went into the hospital for a hysterectomy. Surgeons successfully removed her uterus but left in its place (unintentionally, we can only assume) a fifteen-by-twenty-inch surgical towel. If that wasn't bad enough, doctors opened her up eight more times in the next four months to drain a wound that clearly wasn't healing, not figuring out the fact that the towel was still there.

 Round about the same time, making it a bad month for Canadian hospitals, a hospital in Saskatoon, Saskatchewan, was sued by Rebecca Chinalquay, who was in the hospital to have her baby, which she did. The only problem was that while she was in labor in the delivery room, all the medical staff happened to have gone out. Her baby, Tyler, popped out and, completely unattended, slid off the gurney and onto the floor, starting life with more of a bang than he or his mother would have wanted.

A court case in Japan last year highlighted the agonizing dangers of modifying your delicate bits. The thirty-five-year-old man in question had a steady job and a steady girlfriend but felt that he had been sold a bit short in one particular area. He went to one of Japan's premier cosmetic surgery clinics, the Komuro, where they relieved him of $10,000 and set about enlarging his penis. The next day, the man, in agony, beheld his new penis: S-shaped and with a grossly distorted head. Unable to move without a supply of painkillers, the man underwent several corrective attempts to reshape his penis, and it ended up smaller than before. Fearing that if he went into the hospital he would have to have it amputated, he took his own life. The case revolved around whether there was malpractice, which according to the court there was not, and whether the man should have had more warning about the possible complications of having the operation, which the court ruled he should have, awarding almost $100,000 to his relatives.

Little Megan Parfitt, age three, had an operation to remove some of her milk teeth in Merthyr Tydfil, south Wales, and came home complaining that her tongue hurt. And so it should have— the back of her tongue had been stitched to her gums.

Holly Barbour practices cosmetic surgery in Florida. That's "practice" in the sense of not being very good at it, apparently. She offered a prospective patient a huge discount on a combined face and neck lift, because she had only worked on eyes before and wanted to expand her repertoire. How hard can it be, a simple face-and-neck? Well, after the ten-hour operation (usually it takes five), Barbour's patient ended up with a lump in her face that made a popping sound every time she blinked. The fifty-nine-year-old sued, of course, and was awarded $2.1 million in damages. A sum that probably made her blink. (Pop!)

VANITY AND THE KNIFE

Last year we reported on South Koreans having tongue operations to improve their English speaking and hence get better jobs. Now it appears that young affluent Chinese are pushing the surgical envelope a little further than their Korean neighbors by paying around $6,000 to undergo the Ilizarov procedure in order to become taller. Developed to deal with severe bone fractures, this operation involves months of minute adjustments to a mesh of metal rods constructed around and through the broken bone. And if you are having it done to improve your standing, then the shin or thigh bones have to be broken first. The bones are then pulled apart slightly, allowed to fuse, then pulled again, usually over a six-month period, followed by three months of recovery. At the end of it, the patient gains a few inches in height, and a few notches on the social scale. The rewards for their suffering will, they think, be better jobs and better partners.

It would appear that the concept of virginity is changing, as a craze for having the hymen reinstalled by cosmetic surgery is sweeping Japan. The operation lasts a mere twenty minutes and costs $1,500, but it could be worth it for the women who undergo it, even though many of them are not really in a good position to afford that kind of money. The idea is that being a virgin will help them catch a rich husband. Whatever happened to love and romance?

INSANITY AND THE KNIFE

Long gone are the times when a young man would walk into a hairdresser's carrying a photograph of his idol and ask for a similar hairstyle. In these scalpel-happy days you can ask your friendly neighborhood plastic surgeon to reconstruct you to be the spitting image of your hero, which is how Belgian Emmanuel de Reyghere, thirty, has been spending his time and money. Ironically, Emmanuel's idol is himself no stranger to the surgeon's knife, being the mythically whacky Michael Jackson. After nine operations, the last being that famously tiny, collapsing nose, Emmanuel's face has now become the image of Michael Jackson's, and he says that people recognize him in public. Since he hardly has any friends these days and his girlfriend left him four years ago, he finds this is some consolation. But as Michael's face continues to deteriorate, how will Emmanuel keep pace?

nostalgia and the knife

It can be hard to let go sometimes. . . . Police in Auckland, New Zealand, answered a call from someone who said that they had seen a severed leg tied to the back door of their neighbor's house. The fact that there was a rather large number of flies buzzing around the back door attracted their attention, and, fearing the worst, they called the police. When the police went to the house in question, the owner was easily able to help them with their inquiries: It was his own leg that had just been amputated, and he really wanted to keep it as a memento.

ECCENTRIC

MEDICAL MARVELS

Christiane Kittel, now twenty-four, was a pupil at her local school in Regensburg, Germany, when she suffered a lung embolism. Although emergency surgery saved her life, Christiane never fully recovered and spent the last seven years in a coma. Now Christiane was always a massive fan of gravel-voiced rocker Bryan Adams (who only *sounds* as though he's had a lung embolism) and when her mom found out that he was due to play a gig in their hometown she knew she had to take Christiane along. As the man who made the hit album *Waking Up the Neighbours* played, Christiane herself started to wake from her seven-year slumber. She opened

1995 was a bad year for Peter Sana, of Honolulu, Hawaii. He contracted meningitis and fell into a coma in March of that year. Amazingly, seven whole years later, Peter began to respond to commands from his nurse at the nursing home and soon afterward regained consciousness. Although not in the Rip van Winkle league, Peter has got a lot of catching up to do to cover his seven-year nap—when he lost consciousness, for example, the big news story in the US was the murder trial of O. J. Simpson.

WEIRD

her eyes and started to move in her wheelchair, and when she got back to the clinic she even spoke her mother's name. Christiane's doctor stated that since the Bryan-induced recovery she had not relapsed, adding that "despite the very worst injuries there is always hope." But no hope for her taste in music. . . .

A boy in Calcutta, India, was born without a penis but, by an amazing coincidence, elsewhere in the same hospital, a spare penis came up. A surgeon was operating on a one-year-old boy who had a "troublesome second penis." Once this had been removed it was transplanted onto the baby in an operation claimed to be the first-ever penis transplant. And now the baby has a penis that will always be a year older than he is.

A Taiwanese doctor found the cause of a hacking cough that had been needling his patient for years: Embedded in the man's back, lodged so deep that it irritated his lungs, was a sewing needle. The patient had tried all sorts of cures but had had no relief until Dr. Chiou Ming-hwang spotted something on a chest X-ray. The man's wife remembered losing a needle on their bed several years ago, although the man himself had no recollection of the needle going into him. The needle was removed and the cough vanished with it.

At a routine hospital checkup one day, doctors discovered that the settings in a Japanese woman's pacemaker had mysteriously changed. The manufacturers of the pacemaker sent someone to the woman's house, and an investigation revealed that her rice cooker was the culprit, sending out electric signals that overrode those of the pacemaker. Fortunately for the woman, her heart didn't stop while she was standing near the rice cooker.

A seven-year-old boy in Kazakhstan was admitted to hospital with stomach pains, the cause of which doctors thought initially was a large cyst. But during surgery on Mourat Zhanaidarov they made a very strange discovery indeed. Mourat was carrying inside his body the fetus of his dead twin brother. After seven years, the fetus still had hair, nails, and bones, and although it was not a living organism it was feeding off Mourat's blood supply. Doctors think that had this twin lived, the two boys would have been Siamese twins.

An extremely rare case was brought to the attention of the medical world last year when an eleven-year-old girl from the Thrissur district of Kerala, in southern India, was found to have an extra lung. (That means she had three, in case you weren't sure how many lungs humans normally have.) The third lung was discovered when the girl, Saji, was taken to the hospital with a fever.

In Rabat, Morocco's capital, surgeons operated on a seventy-five-year-old woman to remove what she thought was a tumor that she had had for a long time. The would-be tumor, however, turned out to be a fetus that had been there for forty-six years!

In this case, it was the other way around. The parents of a fifteen-year-old Colombian girl were convinced that she was pregnant and took her to the hospital. She had put on weight and was suffering from abdominal pains and vomiting but denied she was having a baby. After an examination, doctors decided to operate, and found a massive tumor weighing an incredible twenty-six pounds, which took over three hours to remove.

In an accident straight out of a low-rent horror movie, Marcos Parra of Arizona was hit in his car by a drunken driver with such force that his head was literally ripped away from his body, with only the spinal cord stopping his head from being completely severed. Still alive, just, after being rushed to a hospital, eighteen-year-old Parra needed a miracle. And it just so happened that Dr. Curtis Dickman had been practicing and perfecting a new surgical procedure for reuniting severed heads with their bodies, although Parra was the first real-life opportunity he had had to use it. Using two screws and some of Parra's pelvic bone to join the base of the skull to the first cervical vertebra, Dr. Dickman not only saved Parra's life, but he also saved his spine, and instead of being doomed to life in a wheelchair, Parra was able to walk again a few months after surgery.

 A Sri Lankan woman from Walpanee, near Colombo, died in childbirth, leaving her husband to look after the new baby and their eighteen-month-old daughter. The elder child was so used to her mother's milk that she refused to drink formula, so her father, who couldn't bear seeing her so hungry and upset all the time, in desperation offered her his own breast. To his amazement he started producing milk, which his daughter gratefully drank. The phenomenon of the man who could breastfeed his daughter came to the attention of doctors, who pronounced that a man who has a hyperactive prolactin hormone can produce breast milk, so this is not unheard of. Fortunately for the father and his breastfeeding capacity, his younger daughter took to formula.

Chris Brown, thirty-four, of Gloucestershire, had had problems with his lungs since the age of fourteen, when he'd been wrestling with friends in his garden and had swallowed a small twig of leylandii. He'd had breathing difficulties and regularly coughed up blood, but scans failed to show anything. Then one night he woke up coughing, banged himself on the chest, and the twig, after twenty years of being lodged in his lungs, popped out.

THE EYES HAVE IT

Ever tried looking directly into the sun? How many milliseconds can you manage before you pull away, afraid that you've blinded yourself? Then consider the case of a young man in the Indian state of Assam. Twenty-four-year-old Dimbeswar Basumatary

In Thailand, a fifty-three-year-old woman was on her way home from church when she was hit by a truck. The fact that she had been blind since the age of ten may well have contributed to the accident, in which she was knocked down but escaped serious injury. It's a good thing she wasn't killed, anyway, since she wouldn't have been able to enjoy the fact that the accident instantly and completely restored her eyesight.

In what a leading eye doctor referred to as "a miracle," a Norwegian woman with very restricted vision regained her sight during her pregnancy. Mona Ramdal had only 15 percent vision before becoming pregnant, but while she was pregnant her eyesight recovered enough for her to pass her driving test at the first attempt. And by the time her baby was born Mona could see perfectly normally. What the doctors found so amazing was that her retina had been destroyed by toxoplasmosis as a baby, and usually damaged tissue like the retina simply cannot regenerate—except in this wonderful case.

has baffled experts with his ability to stare at the sun for hours at a time. Conventional wisdom holds that looking directly into the sun for more than just ninety seconds will cause permanent retinal damage; yet for the last five years Basumatary has spent whole days at a time gazing at the sun and, according to astonished ophthalmologists who have examined him on several occasions, has suffered no damage to his eyesight. He even claims to derive energy from the sun in this way.

MEDICAL MADNESS

At the time of writing, the SARS virus was a major concern in China, with strangers being refused entry to villages and many people wearing surgical face masks to avoid catching the illness. In southern Taiwan at one stage, face masks couldn't be had for love or money and someone had the bright, if not necessarily medically sound, idea of wearing a bra . . . on his face, that is. One man, his face buried in a red bra cup, spoke of the difficulties of finding masks in the pharmacies, while a small bra factory had its workers cutting bras in half and sewing on straps to make the cups face-friendly. Did they work? No one can say. Did anyone feel like a boob wearing one? Possibly.

An unnamed doctor in the west of England was hauled up for a disciplinary hearing because he refused to certify a patient for a smear test for cervical cancer. Since the patient is a man, the doctor felt he had a case. The patient, however, is convinced he is a hermaphrodite, even though, according to the doctor's examinations, there is no evidence of this, and he has fathered a child. Advised to follow a policy of humoring the patient, the doctor said he would do so as long as someone could show him how to perform a pap smear on a thirty-four-year-old male.

WEIRD CONDITIONS

A Romanian soldier collapsed on the parade ground and went into uncontrollable convulsions. Following exhaustive tests at a military hospital, doctors proclaimed that Adrian Busureanu, twenty-one, was suffering from acute sexual frustration. A spokesman said: "He became feverish, delusional, and finally hysterical after being apart from his girlfriend for two months. He was suffering from hysteria induced by sexual frustration." Hmm. With ten months left of his compulsory military service, it seems likely to us that he may have been looking for an early reprieve.

Sixty-three-year-old Alan Todd from Newcastle had seen various doctors over a forty-year period without anyone finding out just why it was that he would faint and collapse at the sudden sound of the telephone, alarm clock, or doorbell. Finally, experts at Newcastle's Royal Victoria Infirmary discovered that when Mr. Todd experienced a shock his heart simply switched off, leaving him brain-dead for up to thirty seconds. Since this happened up to seven times a day, it was a miracle he was still alive. Now Mr. Todd has a pacemaker programmed to kick-start his heart if it stops beating for more than 1.5 seconds.

STRANGE

MEMORY LOSS

Alice Perley, a homeless woman, trudged into the chic offices of brokerage firm A. G. Edwards and Sons in Nashville, Tennessee, and spoke to the first person she saw—one Michael Guess, a financial analyst waiting by the elevator—saying that she thought she recognized the name of the company and that she had a feeling she had investments with them. Guess decided to go along with her story, despite the fact that she was clearly a bag lady, and called head office to check up on her name. It turned out that not only was Ms. Perley a genuine holder of investments with the company, but that she had been wandering the streets for eight years. A college graduate with a degree in chemistry, she had disappeared from her home in Kentucky after a painful divorce, got off a flight during a stopover at the Nashville airport, and had lived in the woods, on the streets, and in shelters for the next eight years despite frantic and thorough searches by her family. Eventually her memory had been jogged by the company name. Ms. Perley's brother in North Carolina was contacted by the brokerage firm; he spoke to his long-absent sister and arranged to come to Nashville and take her home at last.

Two days after their wedding, Sean McNulty and Amy Henry of Austin, Texas, arrived at a Houston airport ready to jet off to Italy for their honeymoon. As they were about to board the flight, Sean said he had to go back to the car to get his wallet. He did not return. Sean was discovered three days later a few miles from the airport, lying on the ground outside a closed hotel. As police questioned him, it became apparent that he had forgotten his name, his new wife, and where he had just been, and despite extensive medical tests including brain scans and a psychological examination, doctors could not fathom the cause of his total memory loss. As time went by it transpired that Sean had in fact no memory of anything about his life or himself before being picked up and taken to the hospital. He didn't know what his favorite foods tasted like and he was scared by telephones because he had no idea what they were. Strangely, Sean had suffered a temporary memory loss a couple of weeks earlier, returning home from work complaining of nausea and dizziness and not knowing who Amy was; he slept intermittently for thirty-six hours before his memory returned on that occasion.

OVERREACTION

The Japanese language is pretty weird, in many ways, not all of which we can go into here. But one aspect is relevant to this story: In Japanese there are "honorifics"—bits that are added on to a person's name to show respect for the person to whom you are talking. Getting them right is important, and more important to some than others. Takayuki Niimi, thirty-two, failed to use the right honorific when he spoke to an acquaintance of his, Ryuji Sakamoto. Sakamoto punched Niimi to the ground and stabbed him in the face four times with his umbrella; Niimi died later in the hospital. It is not known if Sakamoto used the correct honorific while stabbing Niimi to death.

Last year we saw how a pointless argument over who had the best surname led to senseless violence. This may be even more trivial; see what you think. In New Jersey, Emmanuel Nieves and his friend Erik Saporito were chatting and the conversation turned to their bottoms, and more specifically the hairiness of them. A full-blown argument ensued as to whose buttocks were the hairiest, and Nieves became so incensed that he pulled out his knife and slashed Saporito with it (on the head, not across the buttocks). We don't know if Saporito turned the other cheek when attacked, but if he did it was probably the hairiest.

cutting your nose off to spite your face

The owner of an ancient pub went over the top in a very big way during some New Year's celebrations. Having suffered the humiliation of being refused a drink by his own staff because they were closing up, Robert Tyrell, owner of the charming sixteenth-century North Star Inn in the village of Steventon, Oxfordshire, went and found a mechanical digger (at 3:45 A.M.) and rammed the building, demolishing part of it. Tyrell's timbered pub had a collapsed roof and damaged walls after the attack, and he was charged with criminal damage.

A man overreacted in a Catholic church in Philadelphia when he was frustrated in his attempt to light a candle. What pushed George Johnson over the edge was the fact that his lighter wouldn't work, so he went on a rampage, as you do, decapitating statues, destroying about one hundred candles and cracking a marble lectern with a four-foot brass candlestick.

The city of New York passed a ban on smoking in bars and restaurants at the beginning of April, to, predictably, a very mixed reception. It didn't take long for some totally unnecessary violence to erupt as result—just two weeks, in fact. A security man at a bar in the East Village was stabbed to death after he asked a customer to put out his cigarette. The customer refused, the bouncer went about ejecting him from the bar, and, in the scuffle that followed, was stabbed fatally in the stomach. Proof that smoking kills?

WANTON VIOLENCE

A bingo club in south Wales was forced to ban two grandmothers after a senselessly violent episode in which Sandra Fry, fifty-five, attacked Lynn Want, fifty-eight, because she was in the "lucky chair." Fry was incensed to see her rival sitting in what was supposed to be a "lucky" seat in the club. So she walked up to her and punched her in the face. Security staff had to pull her off as five hundred other bingo players watched in amazement. Ms. Want needed hospital treatment for a broken nose and two black eyes, while on her life ban from Bridgend's Castle Bingo Hall Sandra Fry said, "Even a murderer doesn't get life." No, dear, but you could get a life.

In the state of Massachusetts a seventy-nine-year-old man went onto a golf course to try to find just one abandoned golf ball to give to his grandson. As harmless an act as this sounds, it was in fact a very bad move indeed. He unwittingly upset a certain Robert Carnathan, whose regular ball-collecting patch it was. There was a disagreement that ended with Carnathan's beating the older man to death.

Where was the dignity? Where was the respect for the dead? Two families at a cemetery in Bulgaria, both burying mothers, were subjected to an awful display of unseemliness when a battle broke out between rival undertakers. The men were fighting over a recent court ruling that had ended one of their monopolies on digging graves in Razgrad cemetery. Mourners were forced to run for cover as Evgeni Draganov, of Razgrad, lunged at Stefan

Had they no shame? At a school in southern India all hell broke loose as two male teachers who both liked the same female teacher completely lost it and started a scrap in the playground. With the school's five hundred pupils looking on, the two love rivals rolled on the ground, threw stones and mud at each other, and, horror of horrors, pulled each other's hair. The school was closed down while there was an inquiry into the teachers' behavior. As a spokesman pointed out, they didn't set a very good example.

Petrakiev, from the nearby town of Velev, with a shovel after Mr. Petrakiev threw a clump of mud at his head. The fracas ended when one of the combatants fell into an open grave. As one of the mourners said, the bloodied, muddied men in black had ruined a solemn occasion.

A COLLECTION OF RAGES

We always seem to get a wide range of rage reports here at *Another Weird Year*. Last year there were gems like checkout rage and snow-shoveling rage. This year's crop is equally good. . . .

Jeep rage

A resident of Venice Beach, California, is enraging local owners of SUVs (sport-utility vehicles), those pointlessly macho urban jeeps that are used for nothing more rugged than shopping and cruising the streets. Amy Alkon calls herself an "ethical fascist" and leaves a card under the windshield wipers that reads: "Road-hogging, gas-guzzling, air-fouling vulgarian! Clearly you have a small penis or you wouldn't drive such a monstrosity. For the adequately endowed, there are hybrids or electrics." The card has no name on it but there is a phone number, and drivers who call it hear another message abusing their choice of vehicle.

mailbox rage

In the town of Lexington, Kentucky, a postman had been regularly leaving the door of George Krushinski's mailbox open and Krushinski got angry. Very angry. He planted small bombs in his mailbox and in the postman's van, along with a note: "I've warned you bastards . . . about leaving my mailbox open . . . now you will pay."

Potato rage

In a field near Ansbach in Germany a farmer was incensed when he saw a rival plowing what he thought was his land. He had planted a crop of potatoes on land he had leased, and when he saw another farmer working the land he leapt onto his tractor, drove up to his rival, and rammed him head-on. The other farmer didn't back down, though, and rammed the first man's tractor, and they carried on like a couple of, er, rams, until both tractors were destroyed.

Humming rage

In Illinois, Sheila Raven Lord lost control of her temper when a companion was humming a Megadeth song louder than the Celine Dion song that she was listening to. She stabbed him with a steak knife.

Cookie rage

Laura Smith, of Michigan, flew into a violent rage at a cookie store in a shopping mall when she realized that there were no choc-chip macadamia nut cookies left. She threw a large box of napkins at the assistant, then punched her.

Travel

AIRLINE STORIES

There was something strange going on at the International Airport on the Pacific island of Saipan. A Thai, Chaseeraporn Bonchurigit, set off the metal detector and was given a cursory search in the female "pat-down area." Nothing metallic was found, so she was taken back to the boarding gate, and once again the alarm sounded as she walked through. This constituted a stage one alert, and Bonchurigit was taken away and asked to undress. It was at this point that she was forced to come clean: She was a she-male, not a female, and what had been setting off the metal detectors were her testicle piercings, which she had forgotten to remove before checking in.

A flight attendant on a Northwest Airlines flight had had enough of the antics and noise of one particularly trying nineteen-month-old baby. So Daniel Reed slipped a little something into the apple juice the baby's mother ordered. Unfortunately for Mr. Reed, she took a sip of the juice before allowing the little imp to drink it, and decided it tasted funny. She poured some of the juice into a container and had it tested later. The test results showed the presence of a drug called Xanax, a sedative.

As airliners cruised in over Luton airport, north of London, pilots tuning in to receive landing instructions were hearing not the calming tones of an air traffic controller, but the squalling of a baby. Eventually, after twelve hours of tracking the frequency, traffic controllers marched up the garden path of Lisa Spratley to tell her that the baby monitor she was using to listen to her infant daughter, Freya, was transmitting on the same frequency as their own equipment.

Human vampire refugee in-flight stories (okay, there's only this one)

An Albanian man, on a special flight of refugees being deported from Germany to Kosovo, tried to choke an air hostess on the Montenegro Airlines plane. She had asked him what he would like to drink, to which he replied, "Your blood," and tried to throttle her with his shoe laces. His blood-drinking ploy was foiled by other passengers and airline employees, who quickly came to the air hostess's rescue.

YUCKY TRAIN STORIES

Last year we noted a woman sitting on the toilet being blasted from beneath with raw sewage. This year it was the turn of a Norwegian on a train. The man, from the town of Fredrikstad, was bent over the sink, about to wash his hands, when a jet of sewage shot up through the plughole. Although he tried to block the flow with his hands, his face, hair, and sweater were liberally doused with the effluent. And his hands, too, which of course he had been trying to wash in the first place. We think he probably kicked up a bit of a stink about it.

Rail staff in Slovakia made a gruesome discovery on inspection of an express train that had traveled from Warsaw, in Poland: There was a human leg stuck to the front of it. A man had been hit by the train earlier in the journey, but apparently no one had noticed that one of his legs had been sliced off. The spokesman for the Slovak Railway Police said that the leg would be stored at a local hospital until the victim's family asked for it back to be buried alongside the rest of its owner.

OFF-ROAD DRIVING

If you have an off-road vehicle, then you want to drive it off-road, right? But when a thirty-seven-year-old woman drove into the Ginger Inn Chinese restaurant in Durham, North Carolina, in her Honda SUV and continued driving around the dining room, she was perhaps taking the term "off-road" just a little bit too literally.

If you can't afford a massive, gas-guzzling off-roader, then take a page out of the book of Melodie Morsicato of Connecticut. In her dinky little Nissan Stanza, forty-five-year-old Melodie crashed through the front door of a Target store at 4 A.M. and enjoyed herself by driving around the store for a while, eventually crashing in the store's lawn and patio department for the real country feel.

GREAT ESCAPES

After a big night out on the booze in the town of Auburn in Indiana, Chad Dillon, twenty-four, decided to sleep it off in a garbage bin. Maybe it seemed like the logical thing to do at the time, but the comatose Dillon was picked up by a garbage truck along with the rest of the contents of the bin. He was compacted not once but three times, his screams from inside the truck being heard during the third compacting. Dillon was treated for head, chest, and arm injuries and was described as "lucky to be alive."

An Ecuadorian family left their country and walked together across the border into Chile. What Jorge and Soledad Jaramillo and their three children did not know was that they were walking through a military zone to make their illegal entry into Chile and that they had spent an entire day walking across a minefield. When they arrived at a Chilean military checkpoint the guards couldn't believe that the Jaramillos had not been blown up, and the family all wept when they realized just how incredibly lucky they had been. Several illegal immigrants have lost feet or legs trying to enter Chile through the same area.

A young couple had been out clubbing in the Cornish town of Newquay and retreated to a secluded spot for a bit of intimacy. Cuddling up together at the aptly named Lusty Glaze beauty spot, gazing at the moon from their clifftop vantage point, they were in a passionate clinch when the girl slipped and plunged one hundred feet down the cliff onto the beach below, landing behind a beachfront shop. The twenty-two-year-old suffered not one single broken bone, which paramedics put down to the fact that she was "very relaxed" when she fell.

Good luck and quick thinking combined to save teenager Joe Thompson of Blue Springs, Missouri. Thompson was involved in a car crash that catapulted him twenty-five feet up into the air; the good-luck factor was that he was launched upward near a telephone wire, which he then had the presence of mind to grab onto as he whizzed by. Thompson held tight for twenty minutes before someone passed and he called down, asking them to switch off his car engine. And to get help.

 There I was, thinking that cosmetic surgery was generally pointless, when a story came from the home of pointless cosmetic surgery to prove me wrong. A Brazilian woman, shot in the crossfire between police and drug dealers in Rio de Janeiro, was saved by her silicone breast implants. Although she tried to hide when the shooting started, Jane Selma Soares was hit in her ample chest by a bullet. When she got to a nearby hospital, doctors told her that the implants had slowed the bullet down enough to prevent it causing her anything more than a flesh wound. A plastic surgeon was called in to repair Miss Soares's implants and took the opportunity to increase the size of her breasts, presumably for safety reasons.

BAD LUCK

In Garforth, West Yorkshire, a farmer discovered that his truckload of five hundred bales of straw had caught fire. With the straw ablaze, he sensibly drove to the town fire station—to discover that the firefighters were out on an emergency call.

Oooh, unlucky! A seventy-five-year-old woman in Singapore did the polite thing and kept the doors open for a man running toward the elevator. Tough for her, though, as the man turned out to be an armed robber. He held her at knifepoint while he robbed her of a gold necklace and bracelet.

Roy Dennis from Hampshire visited New Zealand for the holiday of a lifetime. It was, but not for the right reasons. First Roy broke his ankle sky-diving and had to go to the hospital. He left the hospital in a wheelchair and got on with his dream vacation, visiting an aquarium, where he was promptly bitten by a poisonous puffer fish, requiring him to go straight for a tetanus shot. The next day Roy's son, whom he was visiting, took him to an adventure park. He was put in his wheelchair in a special car to tour the park, but he and his chair fell out and rolled into a window, leaving him with a broken nose. Back to the hospital again.

Derek Bond was enjoying his retirement, as a respectable seventy-two-year-old should, and he and his wife, Audrey, decided that a wine-tasting holiday in South Africa would be nice. So it was a bit puzzling when, arriving at Cape Town airport, he was questioned by police about his identity. Even more puzzling, and downright scary, when a couple of days later he was taken from his holiday village and arrested. Poor Mr. Bond, an international fraudster (or so said the FBI), with many millions of dollars' worth of scams to his name, was on their "most wanted" list. Protesting his innocence, Mr. Bond was detained for over two weeks before the FBI found the right man, in Las Vegas, who had, many years earlier, used the name Derek Bond on a false ID.

You might expect a hangover after a night in a club, but sunburn? Ten clubbers at a nightspot in Leeds ended up with peeling skin and eye pain after a night on the dance floor at a club called, believe it or not, Flares. It seems a filter had slipped loose from one of the strobe lights and was bangin' out some serious UV, man.

Fifty-five-year-old Mohammed Hadi, a convicted murderer in Iran, was about to be hanged in public for his crime. He had the noose around his neck and was being read to from the Koran in preparation for his execution when he suffered a heart attack, halting the execution in its tracks. Even though Hadi was taken to the hospital and treated, this was truly only a temporary stay of execution. He was told that once he had recovered from his heart attack, the hanging would go ahead as planned.

Good Samaritan, bad Samaritan

A woman in Manchester saw a man lying in the gutter and dialed 999 on her mobile. This good Samaritan waited in her car until she saw the paramedics arrive, then pulled away; just as she did so the man, a drunk, hauled himself to his feet and promptly collapsed again, right under the wheels of her car. Good thing she'd called the paramedics. . . .

 Here's a man who's a real accident-magnet. Romanian Nicolae Tabacu said that he had had enough after he was run over for the seventh time. Walking (or hobbling) disaster area Nicolae has broken every limb except his right hand, and has kept up the spice in his life by being run over by an interesting variety of vehicles. The most recent accident involved a police car, but he has also been hit by a train and a motorbike, while his first accident was courtesy of a bus. This last accident happened within thirty feet of his home. Nicolae was so depressed by the sheer volume of accidents befalling him that he said he would rather this one had taken his life. Stay out on the streets, Nicolae, it's only a matter of time.

 In surely one of the worst bad-luck stories of the decade, never mind the year, two sisters were involved in a head-on collision. The weird thing about it was that they were each in their own cars, and they were both on their way to see each other. Sheila Wentworth, forty-five, and her sister Doris Jean Hall, fifty-one, were both driving Jeeps in opposite directions on a rural highway in the state of Alabama. Officials were at a loss to say which car crossed the center line, but the collision was bad enough to kill both women, along with Hall's husband. A grandchild and a nephew were also injured.

A fifty-three-year-old man in Pennsylvania had a little difficulty restarting his truck after stopping at a store, so he began to push it, leaning in through the door. The engine suddenly caught and the truck leapt forward, knocking him down, which was unlucky enough, but then the rear wheels rolled over him. This set the truck off to one side slightly, and the fun began again. Describing a lovely arc, the truck went around in a circle and ran over the poor chap again. It set off once more on its circular mission, but the second impact had turned it a little more, enough for it to come to rest against a fence.

STUPID

Leslie Strickland of Tampa, Florida, hit an alligator while driving her car on a Friday night and went back to the scene of the accident on Saturday morning to see if she could help the creature. She found it, still alive, and loaded it into the back seat of her car and drove it home. There she hosed it down and tried to call the Florida wildlife authorities, while a neighbor kindly informed her that possession of an alligator is a felony in Florida. Ms. Strickland, therefore, loaded the alligator back in to her car and drove off to find a pond she could release it into. The alligator started thrashing around and Strickland lost control of the car, swerving off the road and into a mailbox. With her car stuck in a ditch, Strickland was arrested by police not only for possession of an alligator, but also for walking away from the scene of an accident.

When you go back to your car in the parking lot you always hope that it hasn't been broken into or bumped by another car. It may never cross your mind to worry that you might find your car underneath an airplane, but that's what happened to a German woman in the town of Hagen. Simone Merkel returned to her car to find a Mig 21 fighter jet on top of it—and the jet hadn't even been flying. It had been on display in the parking lot, and a truck crashed into the platform it was on, causing it to slide off onto the nearest car—Simone's—totally crushing it.

FINE ART

Don't think that we're passionate guardians of traditional art forms—we're not. But we would like to bring to your attention some of this year's works of art that were just about as untraditional as you can get.

Korean-born artist Hoon Lee licked yellow cake icing off the twenty-five hundred–square-foot floor of a gallery in Omaha, Nebraska. Lee said he wanted people to look at the icing and feel a certain way about the color yellow.

Mr. Cang Xin of China, on show at the Biennale show in Sydney, Australia, asked visitors to bring him objects of their choice for him to lick. The aim of his "Lick the World" show was, he said, to improve the world's spirituality with his tongue.

Italian artist Piero Manzoni died in 1963, but not before creating a set of limited edition artworks that are having an impact on the art world to this very day. Manzoni produced no fewer than ninety ten-ounce cans filled with his own excrement, bearing the label *merda d'artista* (artist's shit). You might call it crap art, but the Tate Modern this year bought one of the cans for over $40,000, which makes Manzoni's shit, at $4,000 an ounce, more expensive than gold (about $3,000 an ounce). True, there aren't that many of the original ninety cans left—forty-five have exploded (pity the art collector who was holding one at the time in a beautifully manicured hand) since they were "made"—so maybe the Tate Modern spokesman was right when he said, "This was a very important purchase for an extremely small amount of money."

Birgit Hansen, a Dane studying design and fine art in Belfast, put on a show as part of her final-year exams that was, well, rather sick. Her piece was called "Mother Land Father Tongue" and involved her reading aloud from French philosophers and then vomiting into a bucket. Birgit was spattered in fake blood while she performed and there was a musical accompaniment, too, as a "binding element." She said that the piece was "about life, being born, then knowing that also we are going to die."

Still with the nutty Nordics, a Danish art gallery owner ended up in court after an incident that took place at an exhibition in 2000, but that was not resolved at the time. Part of the exhibition was a water-filled food blender with two goldfish swimming in it. Artist Marco Evaristtis's idea was to confront viewers with the idea that the blender was there, with fish, and could be switched on; gallery owner Peter Mayer was responsible for the fact that the blender was plugged into a live electricity supply, so when eventually a member of the public reached over and hit the "on" switch, the poor goldfish met a horrible end. Mayer said that not having the blender connected to an electricity supply would have been compromising the piece's artistic integrity, and refused to pay the fine he was given at the time, so he found himself back in court again last year.

WEIRD

Performance art usually crosses the border into weird art, and here's a fine example: London artist Mark McGowan traveled miles across London by rolling along the ground, singing "We Wish You a Merry Christmas." His motive? To encourage people to be kinder to cleaners at Christmas. To symbolize cleaners he wore rubber gloves, and he wore a raincoat, but no protective gear. So after eight and a half hours of rolling and singing, he had bruised knees and ankles but felt "emotional." McGowan's next performance was scheduled to be as a doormat.

Finding the right medium—the right sort of paper, for example, or the right canvas—for your art is important. Sculptor-painter Antonio Becerra's exhibition in the Chilean capital, Santiago, was entitled "Oils on Dogs," and as is suggested by the title, he painted the pictures featured in this exhibition on the preserved bodies of dead dogs. What's more, he received government funding for his work. Becerra had taken the dogs (already dead) from the streets of Santiago and painted pictures on them in an attempt to reflect the violence and cruelty in society.

MUSIC
Beetlemania

Belgium's Royal Palace isn't known as one of the most fabulous buildings in the world. (Surprised? It is Belgium, after all.) But the straitlaced nineteenth-century palace was given a change of appearance by Jan Fabre, an artist obsessed with insects. Fabre refitted the ceiling of the palace's Hall of Mirrors with beetles—1.6 million jewel scarabs, to be exact. They have iridescent green shells and were acquired for Fabre by entomologists who got them from restaurants in southeast Asia, where they are considered a delicacy. Fabre's assistants in Belgium, a team of twenty-nine, worked for four months solid, gluing the beetles to the ceiling of the Hall of Mirrors.

Plagiarism is an ugly accusation in the world of art or music. The creator of the fun-rock group The Wombles, Mike Batt, is now part of a group called The Planets, and they were accused, by the estate of composer John Cage, of stealing from him. On The Planets's latest album they put out a sixty-second piece of total silence, which was a rip-off of Cage's famous "4' 33"," a piece also of complete silence. Mike Batt said that when Cage's estate threatened to sue, they couldn't say exactly which sixty seconds of Cage's piece The Planets had copied. Batt went on to point out that his piece was better anyway, saying in just one minute what it had taken Cage four minutes and thirty-three seconds to say.

If the audience starts to throw vegetables at this group of musicians, the First Viennese Vegetable Orchestra can easily respond by throwing their instruments back at the audience. The orchestra launched its first tour last year, aiming to bring the special musical sound of vegetables to European audiences, playing instruments that they make themselves out of vegetables, such as a carrot flute or a cucumberophone, which has a cucumber tube and a pepper bell. The orchestra consists of eight musicians, one sound technician, and, for the final part of the show when the vegetables are turned into a soup to be shared with the audience, a cook. It doesn't take the musicians long to make their instruments for the next concert: half an hour for the carrot flute, fifteen minutes for the cucumberophone. They dig deep into the world of vegetables for their instruments, using celeriac (for bongos), aubergines (for cymbals), and pumpkins (for drums) as well as carrots and cucumbers. And what do they play? Their music, amplified by special microphones, takes in styles as varied as classical music, free jazz, and experimental music. And when it's all over, the soup is prepared and the audience gets to taste what they've heard.

CLAIRVOYANTS

A Romanian man serving a prison sentence for armed robbery had a dream in which he was told that he could save the life of a particular woman. Dorel Vidican, thirty, asked to help Diana Moldovan, thirty-eight, after seeing her case on TV: Moldovan was dying from kidney failure and was in desperate need of a kidney transplant. Vidican was given permission, and doctors discovered that his tissue was 100 percent compatible with the dying woman's—a one in sixteen million chance. Moldovan's life was saved, and Vidican's astounding dream led to his being granted a presidential pardon for his crime.

It's the bottom line

A blind German clairvoyant hit the news this year because of the manner in which he reads his clients' future. Ulf Buck works by feel, touching the naked buttocks of his customers to tell their fortune. Thirty-nine-year-old Ulf has been blind since the age of three and says that buttocks have lines just like the palm of the hand, but that the bottom is "more intense." His readings cover personality traits as well as what the future holds, and his clients quickly relax to the idea of having their bottoms felt when they realize that it's easy for them to hide their identity. Not that Ulf does it for any other reason than to help his clients and earn a living; a happily married man, he claims not to get a thrill from his predictive groping.

The landlady of a pub in Staffordshire claimed to be able to tell the future by looking at the froth on a pint of lager. Ann Leatherdale said that numbers became apparent to her as she looked at the foam and that they foretold the results of important football matches and horse races. The froth told her that the England football team would beat Slovakia 2–1 in the qualifying match for Euro 2004, and she stated that she had picked the 2001 Grand National winner, Red Marauder, after staring into the froth. And her vision of the number eight appearing in the tiny bubbles during the World Cup was a clear sign that England would make it to the quarter-finals. So far Mrs. Leatherdale has won $1,000 on bets forecast by the heads of pints of lager.

GHOULS AND GHOSTS

A northern Indian town believed it was being terrorized by a ghost that pinched women's bottoms. More than twenty attacks were reported to police in the town of Biswan, Uttar Pradesh, and women living there started walking around with padded posteriors. It is not clear why the locals thought a ghost was to blame, but victims all claimed to have suffered identical scratch marks from its claws, to have lost consciousness, and woken up feeling dizzy. As the residents started to demonstrate in large numbers at the failure of the police to do something about the attacks, the police inspector remarked, quite reasonably, "We can arrest a man, but not a ghost."

Go-go ghosts

It looks like some ghosts in the state of New Jersey have made their way into a strip club. The staff of the Liquid Assets lounge in South Plainfield said the club's owners spotted inexplicable images on a security video last summer, and paranormal investigators claimed they were the spirit of a dead dancer or the souls of Prohibition-era gangsters. Club workers also said the ghosts moved around beer bottles, tossed the bar's soda gun in the air, and brushed up against people (although they didn't charge a fee for this). Club DJ Sergio Lopez, who sometimes sleeps in the lap-dance room after hours, said one night he was disturbed by a strange whooshing sound. Two doors to the room swung open, he saw a flash of light out of the corner of his eye, and then felt a pressure on his ear and face. That minute-long encounter persuaded him to take a video camera the next time he slept there, and his tape captured strange lights dancing around him. An angry spirit? A publicity stunt? Who knows.

It was a dark December night. On the A3 road near Guildford, in Surrey, at about 7:20 P.M., several motorists saw the headlights of a car suddenly swerve off the road at speed and immediately phoned the police to report the accident. But when officers arrived at the spot they could see no evidence of a car's having left the road. In the cold light of day, though, they returned to the place and what they found was bloodcurdling. Buried deep in a ditch, covered by brambles, there was indeed a car. But it looked as though it had been there for a while, and inside was the skeleton of a young man, proving that the accident had not happened the night before. It was revealed after forensic tests that the twenty-one-year-old man had gone missing five months earlier, in July. Had motorists that December night

 It's been a weird year along a fifteen-hundred-foot stretch of road in Herefordshire. In the last twelve months no fewer than twenty-six cars have crashed on exactly the same short stretch of the A465, and the drivers involved said that it seemed as though the steering wheel was being gripped and turned against their will by an unseen hand. Sixty years ago there was a fatal accident just there and it looks as though malign influences are still hovering on the road, preying on unsuspecting drivers.

seen a ghostly re-enactment of the first crash, taking place at exactly the same place and time of day? It would seem so. . . .

The *Spectator* is a weekly magazine; one week, as it was being checked by its editors after coming back from the printers, there was a mysterious and unusual printing fault. Where there should have been a cartoon, the frame was completely black. The art editor called up the cartoonist, Bill Scully, immediately to tell him about the production error and that he would of course still be paid for the cartoon, but found that the cartoonist had died that very week.

SUPERSTITIOUS NONSENSE

There's a demand for dead women in certain parts of China. No, it's not a perv thing, it's a spiritual thing. Or a superstitious thing. People in the Shaanxi province believe that single men who die need a wife to settle down with in the afterlife, and in response to the demand, a crime syndicate has apparently been ransacking cemeteries, digging up female corpses and selling them to the relatives of the men. It looks like business was good, too: They were charging up to $4,000 per dead bride (the younger ones were more expensive) and digging up five a night.

The evil associations of the **QUIRKY** number 666 were in evidence at Halls Fine Art auction house in Shrewsbury, Shropshire. Lot number 666 of a sale of collectable ceramics was a 1940s pottery figure of none other than Adolf Hitler. It was a comical caricature, made to poke fun at the Führer, and was a highly collectable piece. But at the last minute, experts discovered that the figure was an excellent fake, and Lot 666 had to be withdrawn from the sale. Is there no end to the destructive power of this accursed number?

An Austrian man turned up in the Turkish town of Edremit to visit his Turkish father but received quite a shock when he was treated in a positively medieval way by the locals. Sascha Michael Mariacher, twenty-eight, liked to show how unconventional he was by having several piercings, including large hoop earrings, dying his hair bright red, and dressing all in black. And while someone looking like that may not attract a second glance in western Europe, to the terrified residents of Edremit he was clearly in league with the devil himself. Or maybe even an alien—public opinion was divided on exactly where he came from. So they threw stones at him, to the extent that police had to take him into custody for his own protection.

Superstition is as integral to sports as pretentiousness is to wine-tasting, and the fans are just as superstitious as the competitors. So when a Florida farmer and goat breeder found that one of his newborn goats had a white marking on its brown coat in the shape of the figure 3, he named it Li'l Dale, after the late great racing driver Dale Earnhardt, who immortalized the number three. And the people came, in the hundreds, from all over Florida to see the goat that bore a divine message about Earnhardt.

If you believe the faithful in the Portuguese town of Murtosa, 155 miles north of Lisbon, their Saint Goncalo has a rare and precious power to heal. His speciality is, apparently, hemorrhoids. Oh, and acne, too. (And he has a sideline in helping women find husbands, which has led to unmarried men and women in the northern town of Amarante giving each other penis-shaped cakes on the day of his festival.) But back to the hemorrhoid cure. The sadly afflicted believe that if they bare their bottoms in front of the statue of Saint Goncalo, then their piles will subside. Probably the only time the Catholic church would look favorably on you mooning one of its icons.

You've heard of Billy the Bass—make way now please for Colin the Talking Carp. For the seven thousand or so who are part of New York City's Jewish Skver sect, a miracle was visited upon them in the fish market. A twenty-pound carp was about to be slaughtered and made into gefilte fish for Sabbath dinner when, according to the two fish-cutters, the carp shouted out in Hebrew. Yes, that's right, the carp shouted out in Hebrew. Luis Nivelo, one of the two witnesses, is not Jewish and doesn't understand Hebrew, and when the fish started shouting he thought it was the devil; his co-worker, Zalmen Rosen, understood Hebrew perfectly and recounted that the carp told him to pray and study the Torah. Rosen then tried to carry on with his slaughter of the fish but injured himself (proof, of course, that this was a very special fish indeed), and the job had to be finished by his Christian co-worker Nivelo. Opinion in the community was divided as to the meaning of this: Some believed it was the soul of a recently deceased local community leader, channeled through the carp; others believed it was God Himself. Not everyone there took it seriously: One gefilte fish company said it was considering changing its slogan to "Our fish speaks for itself."

Officials in Livermore in California got so fed up with breakdowns in the city's sewer system that they made a formal apology to American Indian

Adam "Fortunate Eagle" Nordwell. Fortunate Eagle had laid a curse on the sewer system in 1969 after workers chopped off a part of a totem pole he had donated for the city's centennial celebration. Since then, many residents believed that sewerage problems were due to the curse. It remains to be seen if the apology will have the desired effect.

SUPERSTITIOUS HYSTERIA

It's weird what people will people believe when a rumor starts circulating. . . .

In the Ghazipur district of Uttar Pradesh, in northern India, a man was going around the villages plucking the flesh from his victims with his long claws. At least that was what most of the people of the region believed, and that's what's important. He was described as having long hair and bloodshot eyes as well as claws like a tiger and red and green lights emanating from his body. Villagers were leaving their homes in terror rather than risk having their flesh plucked from their bodies. There had been thirty-six victims, according to the rumor, one of whom claimed to have seen the red and green lights coming from "the monster man." Weddings were canceled, and in the stifling summer heat when everyone typically has to sleep outdoors, people were retreating inside to spend sleepless nights. A team of police officers was trying to identify the man, but with red and green lights coming from him, he shouldn't have been too difficult to find.

"No one can categorically claim to have confronted the Muhnochawa," was the official verdict on a creature said to be behind a series of horrific attacks in the Indian town of Raitha. That didn't stop the populace from giving total credence to the idea that the Muhnochawa was a flying octopus-like creature that attacked people in the face and flew away, leaving hideous scars. It, too, emitted a light (just red, no green). What on earth could be behind the rumors? How about this? "In Raitha, Shakeel, his wife, Umar Jahan, and two sons were sleeping on the terrace when two cat-like animals attacked the adults and fled. Shakeel suffered scratches on his back, which, the police claimed, resembled that caused by a claw." Could that "cat-like creature" with scratchy claws be . . . some sort of cat? Or is that just too obvious?

NON-SUPERSTITIOUS SENSE

A man's firm belief that the voice in his head was rooted in the real world (whatever that is) paid off—eventually. For three months, Alfred Mansbridge of Southampton was visited by a ghostly voice in the night, a small, slight voice that woke him in the early hours of the morning. He couldn't tell where it came from—sometimes it seemed to come from the living room, other times from upstairs. And it always said the same thing: "I won't take the lift down." No one else ever heard it, not even Mr. Mansbridge's daughter Joanne, who visits her father every day, so he recorded the voice to prove it wasn't just inside his head. They noticed that the voice spoke at the same time, just before 2 A.M. every day, and stopped after about fifteen seconds. The story made the *Southern Echo* and even the *Paranormal News*, and exorcism was mentioned, but Mr. Mansbridge refused to believe that there was no rational explanation for the phenomenon, even though by this time he was hardly able to sleep. Eventually a crack team of ghostbusters was called in: the local environmental health staff. And Mr. Mansbridge's faith was justified. On a bookcase in the living room they discovered a Spider-Man watch that Joanne had bought for her young son: The alarm, which plays a catchphrase from the film, was set for 1:55 A.M.

MYSTERY CREATURES

It was a perfect summer day on the beach at Portsmouth in the state of Rhode Island. A group of friends, Dennis Vasconcellos, Rachel Carney, Joey Mailloux, Tracy Roberts, a young child, and another woman were swimming and fishing when Dennis Vasconcellos heard a scream from his girlfriend, Rachel Carney, who was in the sea. She seemed to be saying that something was after her, and Vasconcellos swam out to where she was as fast as he possibly could. What was described as an unknown sea creature—it didn't look like any fish or marine mammal or reptile that anyone could think of—was swimming around Carney. It was described as being about fifteen feet long, with four-inch teeth, greenish-black skin, a white belly, and, as Vasconcellos put it, "a head the size of a basketball." And what was most eerie was that it was lifting its head out of the water and hissing at Carney. Vasconcellos pulled Carney to the safety of the beach, where they tried to fathom just what the creature could possibly be. Vasconcellos and his friend Joey Mailloux are both very experienced fishermen and neither had ever seen anything like it; and the chief aquaculturist at the University of Massachusetts Center for Marine Science and Technology was equally baffled by the description of the serpentine creature.

Every now and then reports of a lake monster surface with enough regularity and volume for a new "Nessie" to be proclaimed. Last year, *Another Weird Year* came across the fact that hundreds of sightseers reported spotting a black monster with a horse-like head in a deep volcanic lake near China's border with North Korea. Stories of a mysterious creature in Tianchi Lake have been around for a long time, apparently, but in the latest sighting the creature appeared just thirty feet from the lake shore, jumping out of the water several times, "like a seal." Local monster fans, unfazed by the skepticism of scientists, who, predictably, pooh-pooh the idea that there is anything there, have started the Tianchi Monster Society.

THE LAST LAUGH

There was a story doing the rounds last year about a waitress who worked at the very classy (not!) restaurant chain Hooter's. Jodee Berry was told that the prize for saleswoman of the month at the Panama City, Florida, branch was to be a Toyota. When she was presented with the prize, she was taken out blindfolded to the parking lot, where those laugh-a-minute funsters she worked for had a toy Yoda for her. Geddit? That's a doll of a *Star Wars* character, which sounds just like a Japanese car. If you're American. It was, according to the Hooter's manager, just a silly old April Fool's joke. Well, Jodee Berry didn't see it like that. She had sold the most beer that month and she wanted her car, so she sued for breach of contract. And after lengthy legal wrangling, guess who eventually had the last laugh? Ms. Berry finished up in the local Toyota dealership picking out the car of her choice, so she was probably the one laughing loudest.

Great prank, shame about the outcome. John Sullivan's neighbors were treated to a New Year exhibition of stunning originality. Almost naked and apparently with his backside on fire, Sullivan streaked down his road in the New Zealand port of Tauranga perched upon a motorized barstool. Mr. Sullivan was the first to admit that he had been drinking, which made his presence on a motorized vehicle a bit naughty—and the flaming backside was a rolled-up newspaper stuck into his underpants and set alight. His neighbors hadn't found Mr. Sullivan's antics amusing and called the police, who arrested him for being on an unlicensed and unregistered vehicle (Mr. Sullivan claims his motorized barstool can reach 50 mph), the end result being a community service charge for Mr. Sullivan.

DJs on 92.3 Extreme radio in Cleveland, Ohio, were offering concert tickets to callers who could guess how many helium balloons it would take to lift certain objects off the ground. They then announced that the next thing they would be tying the balloons to was a cat, and dismayed listeners heard the DJs apparently lose control of the floating feline and ask for help as it disappeared out of the studio window. Over the next three and a half hours spoof reports of the cat's location over the city continued to take in gullible (and outraged) listeners, many of whom called 911 and the local animal protection agency to complain. The DJs finished the joke off in style, saying finally that the balloons had been shot down but that the cat was fine. They later admitted it was all "theatre of the mind."

WEIRD FINDS

It wasn't so much a case of the walls having ears as the lawn having eyes. In the town of Ferguson, Missouri, the children of Mr. Adam Comer found thirteen eyeballs in their back yard. Three other houses

in the neighborhood also had a few eyes scattered in their yards. Police took the eyeballs away for tests, which determined that they came from cows, but no one could say how a total of eighteen eyeballs actually came to be there.

It was just a box lying in a street in the Norwegian capital, Oslo, when two teenagers came across it. Its official appearance stimulated their curiosity, and they wasted no time in opening it. First there was some documentation. Then there was a human brain. A pickled human brain, in fact, preserved in formalin. And the paperwork was a death certificate and an autopsy report. There had been a burglary at Oslo's Ullevål University Hospital, and the thieves had dropped the box as they made their getaway, disgusted that it contained nothing more than the brain and some papers. When the teenagers had gotten over their initial shock, they contacted the hospital and the brain was returned.

Heroes

CONSUMER HERO

Gary Wilke of Wisconsin felt all the frustration of the weak individual in the face of the powerful corporation when the computer he bought for his daughter continually malfunctioned. It still refused to boot up after having been taken back five times for repairs to the Gateway store where Mr. Wilke had bought it. He then took the $2,600 computer into the foyer of the store, produced a large sledgehammer from the trunk of his car, and took out all his frustration on it, smashing it to smithereens; he told the Gateway employees to "Have a good day" and left. The result, apart from his being arrested later at his home on a charge of disorderly conduct, was that he became a consumer hero, with e-mails and phone calls of support coming in from people all over the world, people who also wanted to smash their computers but didn't dare. "It feels good in a way," said Wilke later about his elevation to computer-smashing hero status.

FOLK HERO

Single mother of seven Telma Sueli refused to leave her house, which had been illegally built, as she had nowhere else to go. The owners of the land on which Sueli's house stood won a court order to bulldoze her home and hired Amilton dos Santos to do the job. Dos Santos sat at the wheel of his bulldozer and tried three times to start his engine but burst into tears and was unable to go through with the job. As first the local papers and then the nationals picked up the story and ran with it, dos Santos, who lives in a very similar house with his wife and nine children, became a national hero, and following the publicity uproar Ms. Sueli's condemned house was not demolished.

WEIRD SUPERHERO

The residents of the Brambleside estate in the Northamptonshire town of Kettering can sleep safe in their beds at night knowing that The Phantom is out there—collecting litter. The masked maverick has been spotted on security cameras, armed with a broom and trash bags, his face swathed in a scarf, a cowboy hat tipped low to hide his features. After his nocturnal street-cleaning he leaves messages on bins saying, "Keep Brambleside tidy—best wishes, The Phantom."

Miscellaneous

LIFE'S LITTLE IRONIES

Researchers in Dorset were forced to postpone plans to measure the effects of the wind on 950-year-old Corfe Castle, because, of course, it was too windy to set up the measuring equipment.

A TV news crew went out to run a report on holiday fire safety in Colorado Springs, interviewing the owner of a candle shop. Just two hours later, a faulty candle in the shop started a blaze that gutted four businesses.

Another Weird Year is not really a repository for the sort of newspaper misprints and inappropriate headlines that are frequently gathered in other places, but one tragically ironic example did catch our eye—a flyer that read: "Chester and District Branch of the Alzheimer's Society present—Music to Remember."

And another little gem. Just as the SARS epidemic was starting to look like a major world problem, the Hong Kong Board of Tourism was running an ad in magazines that promised that Hong Kong would "take your breath away." The ad was pulled.

In Waiuku, near Auckland, New Zealand, a desperate hunt for a missing seven-year-old girl took place after her mother came back to the family van from a quick stop to find her gone. The mother of Yona Hou reported her daughter missing and drove around the town in the van looking for her, while a police helicopter was called in and an army of volunteers took part in the search. After six painful hours of fruitless search a sharp-eyed policeman spotted Yona fast asleep in the back of her mom's van.

There was a fire at a factory in Neuruppin, Germany. What did they make at this factory? Fire extinguishers. Did any of them work? No. The fire department had to come and put out the fire with their hose.

A British politician was being filmed for a news interview in London for ITN. Just as he spoke the opening words of his interview, "My name is David Jamieson and I am the minister for road safety," there was a screech of brakes and directly behind him a pedestrian was knocked down by a bus. The interviewer reported that there was a pool of blood on the road but that the pedestrian walked off in a hurry, clutching his head and saying he had a train to catch.

BIZARRE

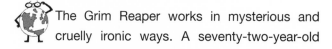 And still on the theme of road safety . . . America's top pedestrian safety expert, Susie Stephens, was in St. Louis to advise at a cycling and walking conference when she was knocked over and killed by a bus. The driver said he didn't see her as he made a left turn.

A twenty-two-year-old man robbed a bank in Cleveland, Ohio, by walking up to a teller, thrusting a gun in his own mouth and threatening to kill himself if he wasn't given the money. Five days later he was shot to death in Akron, Ohio, when he pulled a gun on a police officer.

In the US, a driver and his forty-seven-year-old female passenger buzzed happily along Interstate 94 toward a state border. The passenger was killed when the driver crashed straight into the sign reading "Welcome to Minnesota."

Isn't it strange how nature can point us to deeper truths? In the city of Derby, nature took a hand in redesigning a floral tribute planted to read, in letters two feet high, "Derby in Bloom." Fast-growing shrubs made it read "Derby in Gloom."

The Grim Reaper works in mysterious and cruelly ironic ways. A seventy-two-year-old man plunged to his death from a cliff at Buck's Pocket State Park in Alabama as he threw into the air the ashes of his recently deceased son and overbalanced.

WHAT'S IN A NAME?

Richard James of St. Albans is no longer Richard James. In exchange for a pint of beer, Richard agreed to change his name there and then, in the pub. His friends, who suggested the joke, wrote a variety of names down on a coaster, and then, with the use of a laptop computer and a credit card, paid $80 to transform Richard into Mr. Yellow-Rat Foxysquirrel Fairydiddle. Richard then went on to get a credit card in his new name and informed his bank of his new identity. The fun wore off before too long, but unemployed Richard—sorry, Mr. Yellow-Rat Foxysquirrel Fairydiddle—could not afford, at the time of writing, to change his name back.

A wonderful act of initiative and goodness by an eight-year-old boy prevented a serious train crash in Bangladesh as fifteen hundred passengers sped toward a broken section of track. The little boy was walking to school along the track when he noticed the broken line, so, in a poignant echo of *The Railway Children*, he took off his red shirt, tied it to a stick, and waved it madly in front of the oncoming train, which stopped in time. The name of this little angel? Saddam Hussein.

When you're struggling to find an appropriate name for your baby, remember that you can always use the name of the criminal gang of which you are a member. That was the tactic used by a New Zealand couple, who named their son Triple M Rogue, short for the Mighty Mongrel Mob, Rogue chapter. There is a law in New Zealand banning the use of offensive names, so little Triple M Rogue, bless him, may not grow up with that name, although if the gang is as tough as it is supposed to be he may not live that long anyway.

The names of the Lane brothers of New York made it into the news last year when they were profiled in a newspaper report. Elder brother Winner Lane is forty-four, and his younger brother, Loser, is forty-one. It would appear that Loser is something of a winner, having successfully made it as a police detective in the South Bronx. Winner, on the other hand, is more of a loser, with a history of petty crimes to his name.

The name Kalashnikov is a byword for violence these days, as the Kalashnikov assault rifle is a favorite with terrorists and is a regular feature in urban gang warfare. Well, Mr. Mikhail Kalashnikov is still around and, at the age of eighty-three, has expressed remorse for his infamous invention and declared that he wants to rehabilitate his name by joining up with a German company to manufacture Kalashnikov umbrellas.

Naming a child after a national hero is all very well—but what if the hero in question is a horse? An Italian man from the small southern town of Boscotrecase went to the records office while his wife was still recovering from giving birth to their son and registered his baby's name as Varenne Giampaolo—Varenne after the horse considered to be Italy's greatest-ever trotter, and Giampaolo after the horse's jockey. Such is the adulation given to Varenne that it was named Italy's athlete of the year for 2001, but the man's wife was horrified to discover that her choice of name (Christian) had been ditched in favor of the equine name and went to court to fight her case.

Originality was obviously not the strong suit of the Spencers of Wilkes-Barre, Pennsylvania. Four Spencer men were charged by the prosecutor with stealing tires. They were Edgar Spencer, and his son, Edgar Spencer, the father's brother, Edgar W. Spencer and his son, Edgar W. Spencer.

Last year we looked with disbelief and dismay at some of the newer and more frightening names given to children in the US—names like Armani and Timberland and Canon (as in the cameras). This year we'd like to pay tribute to a less materialistic age, as we spotted that a newspaper in California caught up with some of the state's aging hippie population from the '60s and '70s, interviewing people who had legally changed their original given names to full-on, spaced-out hippie creations. Featured were Mr. Climbing Sun, Mr. Shalom Dreampeace Compost, and Mr. Chip. Also located, but unavailable for interview, were Darting Hummingbird Over a Waterfall and Moonbeam. Like, really cool names, man.

It was just too wonderful an opportunity to waste, but waste it she did. In the city of Flint, Michigan, Laura Kah married Scott Boom. And, ignoring how great an impact she could make in life if she chose to hyphenate, she carried on as plain Laura Boom.

They say Yorkshire people are dour and practical, maybe even unimaginative. But not one Yorkshireman in Halifax. He's a steward at Halifax Rugby League Club, and he so loves supporting and stewarding at Halifax Rugby League Club that he changed his name by deed poll to Halifax Rugby League Club.

And what about naming your child after a superhero? A Swedish couple applied to name their son "Staalman," the Swedish version of Superman, after their comic-book hero, but were told by authorities in Stockholm that they could not, saying that it was not an appropriate name.

Mr. Lee Twinn of Chingford, London, was overjoyed when his partner, Karen, gave birth to twin girls. There had been twins in the family, but not on the Twinn side, so Mr. Twinn didn't really think he'd be the father of twins. But now he is.

Ikea's furniture names. You're starting to chuckle already. There was "Bra," which the English-speaking world found titillating. And last year the name of a children's wooden bed caused problems in Germany. The bed was named "Gutvik" after a small town in Sweden, but all advertising in Germany with that name on had to be recalled after it turned out that the word meant "good f**k" in German.

UPTIGHT CITIZENS

Some desperately uptight neighbors really do have far too much time on their hands. Life's too short to be phoning the police and complaining about an "inappropriate snow figure," isn't it? But apparently not in Kent, Ohio, where police officers arrived at a woman's house after a neighbor took exception to her realistic snow-woman. Crystal Lynn had gone for a bit of realism by adding extra blobs of snow for breasts, but a neighbor complained to the police. Her reward for her creativity was to be told by police to remove the blobs. Crystal refused but compromised by draping a tablecloth around her snow-woman's upper body. Police Captain James Goodlet said that it was the first time there had been a complaint about an indecent snow figure in the whole of his twenty-six years of police work. Really?

STUPID

They say an Englishman's home is his castle, and here's proof of that rather overprotective attitude. There was an early-morning house fire in the Solihull district of Birmingham, to which firefighters were called. As they bravely tackled the blaze, people living in neighboring properties asked them to please keep the noise down.

ALTERNATIVE EDUCATION

In the idyllic mountain region of southern Austria, Europe's first school for witches and wizards opened. A serious school, this is, catering for three classes of students. Last year up to fifteen sorcerer's apprentices were taught astrology, magic, history of magic, meditation, and divination and later had to put their theoretical studies into practice, preparing potions, making talismans, and performing rituals. The school's director, Andreas Starchel, who also calls himself Dakaneth, says the school aims to pass on ancestral knowledge that is in danger of being forgotten and restore contact with nature. And of course the school is in no way cashing in on the Harry Potter phenomenon.

Is this such a bad approach to education? A Minnesota Sunday school teacher was convicted of a misdemeanor for his advice to a teenage boy with a heavy mastur-  bation habit: The thing that would remind him of what was the right thing to do when tempted, according to the teacher, was to write "What would Jesus do?" on his penis. How long before the caution gets swiftly wiped off, though?

POO

Doesn't have to be weird, but sometimes it is. Bill Jenness was faced with a bill of $2,800 to carry out correct disposal of his cat's waste after alarms detected its radioactivity at an incinerator. Jenness was traced from an envelope with his address on it that was in the same bit of trash and hit with a huge disposal bill. He had been advised by the vet who treated his cat to flush the offending poo down the loo, but he threw it out with the trash to make sure his drains didn't get blocked. Jenness's cat, Mitzi, had been suffering from hyperthyroidism, which the vet treated using radioiodine, a drug that renders the cat slightly radioactive for several weeks. The treatment, at Radiocat, plus the waste disposal came to a total of $5,000, but Mr. Jenness said he didn't mind paying because he knew he had not followed instructions, and anyway, his cat was getting better.

In a scene reminiscent of that Hollywood classic *The Poo That Time Forgot*, biologist Gerry Kuzyk, exploring a very remote area of the Yukon, came across a half-mile-long, eight-foot-high stretch of brown stuff. Being a biologist, he swiftly identified this gargantuan deposit as being caribou poo. His conclusion was that there were centuries of deposits that had been frozen, creating a sort of poo glacier, and that they had recently thawed.

BEAUTY QUEENS

It's a world of beauty, perhaps, but it's also full of rivalry, jealousy, and plain bitchiness.

Blondes have more fun and redheads have more insults hurled at them. In Britain the term "ging" is never complimentary, and we suspect attitudes are similar in many other countries. However, like the popularity of Nicole Kidman, there are always exceptions to the rule, and a notable one has emerged in Germany, where Babett Konau confounded experts and critics to become the first-ever Miss Germany with ginger hair. And she was crowned Queen, having beaten twenty-one non-redheads in the town of Rust.

In Georgetown, Kentucky, police charged the organizer of the Georgetown College beauty pageant with assault. It appeared that Kathy Wallace had beaten up contestant Keaton Lynch Brown, eighteen, when it came to her talent presentation. Ms. Brown showed off her chosen talent by lassoing a stuffed pig on stage. Ms. Wallace took exception to that, and there was an altercation based on whether lassoing a stuffed pig was ladylike, and things escalated from there.

TATTOO STORIES

A tattoo is for life. Last year we noted tattoos of Led Zeppelin lyrics and Russian presidents. What artistic wonders have people put on their bodies this year?

Truck drivers are often deeply in love with their work, and their trucks, the freedom to roam the open road, cutting off small cars, trundling up the middle lane of the highway slowing down the rest of the traffic, eating in greasy spoons three times a day . . . what a life. Thirty-five-year-old trucker Steve Hood even had a foot-square image of his beloved forty-ton $150,000 DAF XF truck etched into his back in a nine-hour marathon tattooing session. And the tattooist was so impressed by the unusual nature of the request that he dropped his typical $500 fee to just $100. Trucks have a way of getting under your skin. . . .

Having a tattoo is supposed to enhance your life, or at least give you a meaningful memory. In the strange case of Richard Goddard Jr., a tattoo led to all sorts of trouble. The story begins in 2002, when his local radio station in Davenport, Iowa, offered $30,000 a year for up to five years to any listener who would have "93 Rock," the station's ID, tattooed on his forehead. Goddard and his step-father, David Winkleman, both took the offer at face value and had the tattoo done. Subsequently, the radio station allegedly went back on the deal, and Goddard got a lot of news coverage. Goddard, his already rather messy life further in tatters, was staying in a trailer with John and Mary Rushman, and constantly complaining about the tattoo, the money, and the radio station, and just as frequently threatening suicide. It seems that the couple were so sick of his unabated whining that they slung a rope over a ceiling beam, tied a noose around his neck, and tried to hang him, hitting him in the face with a hammer, too (and maybe screaming "Stop going on about that ****ing tattoo!" as well).

Carl Whittaker's dad, Barry, had some impressive tattoos. Unusually, he had them done only when he found out he was terminally ill. Barry, from Queensland, Australia, had four done on his back and arms, and asked in his will for them to be removed from his body after his death and preserved. Son Carl honored his dad's final request and had the skin removed by a taxidermist and preserved by a tanning company. Now the pieces of his dad's skin, complete with tattoos, are framed and hang in Carl's dining room, the central tattoo being a large image of an eagle entangled with a snake. Beats a photo any day. **ODD**

Tattooing is supposed to be an art—of sorts. But would you have your tattoo etched upon your skin for the rest of your life by a robot? An Austrian electrician invented the world's first tattooing robot and underwent some rather erratic (and permanent) experimental attempts. Niki Passath, twenty-five, then unveiled his creation, called Freddy, at a high-tech fair in Vienna. Freddy has a computerized brain that never plans the same design twice, so those volunteers brave enough to risk their skin to Freddy went away with a tattoo that was unique in conception and design.

WEIRD

A retired nurse from Hampshire had the words "Do Not Resuscitate" tattooed on her chest. The eighty-five-year-old woman also had a tattoo of a heart with a bar through it, a bit like a no-smoking sign. She said that the tattoo was to stop paramedics from trying to resuscitate her if she had a heart attack. During her long nursing career she had seen too many heart attack victims resuscitated who would have been better left to die, she said.

HIDING IN THE CUPBOARD

You can hide in the cupboard, but *Another Weird Year* will find you.

The little country of Swaziland has a state-run radio service—with probably not the biggest expense account. This may have been why their reporter on the spot in Baghdad during the Iraq war was spotted broadcasting from a broom cupboard in the capital's parliament building. MPs in Swaziland said they saw Phesheya Dube there, while the host of the radio program he was reporting for was asking after his safety and advising him to find somewhere to hide from missiles. Information Minister Mntomzima Dlamini promised to investigate the matter, while the radio station refused to comment.

Halfway through a murder trial the murder victim was found—alive, well, and living in a cupboard—four years after she had gone missing and two years after her family had given her up for dead. Natasha Ryan had been living with her boyfriend just half a mile away from her family home in northern Queensland, Australia. When Ryan vanished she was just fourteen, so her relationship with her boyfriend, who was twenty-two at the time, was illegal. Meanwhile, Leonard Fraser, a convicted killer, had been accused of killing Ryan and three other women in the area at around that time. Moreover, the prosecution alleged that Fraser had actually confessed to a fellow prisoner that he had killed Ryan and buried her body under a mango tree. A tip-off to the police during the trial triggered a raid and Ryan was found in the cupboard, while her boyfriend denied all knowledge of her whereabouts. Fraser was cleared of all charges relating to the murder. Naughty Natasha was later charged with wasting police time.

NUDITY

People taking their clothes off for none of the normal reasons. . . .

Last year, a national farming organization in Sweden made the by now fairly predictable step of trying to change the public image of farmers by publishing a risqué calendar featuring tasteful photographs of hunky, bare-chested young men to put an end to the idea that Swedish farmers were just grumpy old men with hats. A year later a group of real Swedish farmers, grumpy old men in hats every one of them, from the small town of Rimbo, posed naked with their modesty covered by chainsaws and shovels. Tasteful and attractive it was not, and Ann Linden, whose idea the first calendar was, criticized their jumping on the nude Swedish farmer calendar bandwagon and feared that it would undo her good PR work. Something tells me the grumpy old men in hats just don't care.

The boss of a nightclub in Cologne in Germany came up with a novel idea to reduce the "atmosphere of aggression" that often prevailed at his club: naked bouncers. And before your mind's eye is filled with disturbing visions of large, hairy, naked men patrolling the line, boss Philipp Sommer's idea was to have naked women as bouncers. Not only are things now a lot less violent, but he has also doubled the club's turnover.

The things businessmen get up to when they are away from home. A man from the state of Idaho on a business trip in Massachusetts was arrested for jogging in the nude. He had parked his car near a hospital in the town of Burlington and put on his running shoes and absolutely nothing else. He was seen by security guards at the hospital running around and doing exercises. He was charged with indecent exposure; police said afterward that he was talking rationally about computers and didn't seem to have any mental problems.

The start of the monsoon season in parts of northern India is such an important time that if the rain is late something has to be done to hurry it along. The rain didn't appear to be coming last year, so people in the states of Uttar Pradesh and Madhya Pradesh turned to the age-old ritual of plowing in the nude at night. And that was just the women (we don't know if the menfolk were allowed to watch). It was an attempt to appease the Hindu rain god Indra, who, according to the naked women, was angry with the communities because they were arrogant. Note that the rain god is male: The naked women had their prayers answered, and the monsoon came shortly afterwards.

hello, sailor!

A very naughty sailor upset diners enjoying a pleasant evening meal at a waterside restaurant in Stratford, Connecticut. Dale Hallquist, forty-three, guided his boat to the rocks just in front of the restaurant and climbed onto them. The fact that he was totally naked came as something of a shock to the diners, but they were then further horrified when he began to shout, capping his display by defecating on the rocks. That's not nice when you're having your dinner. When the harbormaster confronted him, Hallquist went back to his boat and encased his body in plastic wrap. Not a great improvement. Finally police took him into custody.

SORRY ABOUT THE DELAY

The Indian Post Office took nine years to deliver a letter, and as is so often the case in these stories, the recipient lived only about a mile away from where the letter was posted. C. P. Pathre also had to pay for the privilege of receiving the nine-year-old missive because postage rates had gone up during that time. Pathre was preparing a letter of complaint to the post office, which he said he would deliver by hand.

A woman in Connecticut returned a library book that was nearly ninety-four years overdue. Kelly Woodward discovered the book (a collection of plays) in her parents' attic. It was due back at Vernon Public Library in May 1909, and the overdue fine amounted to $800. However, the library directors very graciously decided to waive the penalty.

Not True, Unfortunately

It's amazing how much shelf life these urban legends have. This one was sent to me as a "true" story by one of my stringers/helpers, and I included it in the manuscript after a swift check. Fortunately another check revealed the story to date from 1998, and now it seems it first appeared in 1997! Here's the story:

Two men—Thurston Poole, thirty-three, of Des Arc and Billy Ray Wallis, thirty-eight, of Little Rock—were seriously injured when their pickup truck left the road and struck a tree near Cotton Patch on State Highway 38. The accident occurred as the two men were returning to Des Arc after a frog-gigging trip. On an overcast Sunday night, Poole's headlights malfunctioned and the two men concluded that the headlight fuse had burned out. A replacement fuse was not available, but Wallis noticed that the .22 caliber bullet from his pistol fit perfectly into the fuse box next to the steering wheel column. Upon inserting the bullet, the headlights again began to operate properly and the two men proceeded eastbound toward the White River Bridge. After they had traveled approximately twenty miles, just before they crossed the river, the bullet apparently overheated, discharged, and struck Poole

With this story, again sent to me in all good faith, I immediately smelled a rat: It would seem that people started getting wind of it around about 1996, and it was simply made up. For fun. Well, I think it stinks.

A terrible diet and a room with no ventilation are being blamed for the death of a man who was killed by his own gas. There was no mark on his body, but an autopsy showed large amounts of methane gas in his system. His diet had consisted primarily of beans and cabbage (and a couple of other things). It was just the right combination of foods. It appears that the man died in his sleep from breathing the poisonous cloud that was hanging over his bed. Had he been outside or had his windows been open, it wouldn't have been fatal, but the man was shut up in his nearly airtight bedroom. According to the article, "He was a big man with a huge capacity for creating this deadly gas." Three of the rescuers became sick and one was hospitalized.

in the right testicle. The vehicle swerved sharply to the right, exiting the pavement and hitting a tree. Poole suffered only minor cuts and abrasions from the accident but will require surgery to repair the other wound. Wallis sustained a broken clavicle and was treated and released. "Thank God we weren't on that bridge when Thurston shot his (intimate parts off) or we might have been dead," stated Wallis. "I've been a trooper for ten years in this part of the world, but this is a first for me. I can't believe that those two would admit how the accident happened," said Snyder. Upon being notified of the wreck, Lavinia, Poole's wife, asked how many frogs the boys had caught.